SUCCESS PRINCIPLES WORKBOOK

MILLIONAIRE SUCCESS HABITS

Get Into The Minds and Work Ethics of The Wealthiest In The World

LEWIS CLARK

Table of Contents

PART 1 5
Chapter 1: Seven Habits That Will Make You Successful......................6
Chapter 2: 10 Habits to Start Right Now...11
Chapter 3: 10 Habits to Change Your Life...17
Chapter 4: 10 Habits of Warren Buffet..24
Chapter 5: 7 Habits To Change Your Life 29
Chapter 6: 10 Habits of Unsuccessful People..34
Chapter 7: 6 Reasons your emotions are getting in the way of your success 40
Chapter 8: 10 Habits of Jeff Bezos...44
PART 2 49
Chapter 1: 7 Habits That Are Good For You...50
Chapter 2: 6 Habits of Oprah Winfrey..55
Chapter 3: 5 Ways To Adopt Right Attitude For Success....................60
Chapter 4: *6 Ways To Adopt A Better Lifestyle For Long-Term Success*..........63
Chapter 5: 10 Habits of Lewis Hamilton 67
Chapter 6: *8 Steps To Develop Beliefs That Will Drive you To Success*............71
Chapter 7: *6 Ways On How To Change Your Body Language To Attract Success* 75
Chapter 8: 9 Habits of Highly Successful People 78
PART 3 84
Chapter 1: *6 Tricks to become more aware of your strengths.* 85
Chapter 2: 10 Habits of Elon Musk..89
Chapter 3: *7 Reasons Your beliefs are holding you back.*............................94
Chapter 4: 7 Habits To Start Right Now 98
Chapter 5: *6 Steps To Get Out of Your Comfort Zone*............................. 103
Chapter 6: 5 Habits of Bill Gates 109
Chapter 7: 10 Habits of Jack Ma 114

Chapter 8: 10 Habits of Bernard Arnault... 119

Chapter 9: 8 Habits You Should Have For Life................................... 124

PART 1

Chapter 1: Seven Habits That Will Make You Successful

A man's habits are as good as his lifestyle. Some habits are akin to successful people. The path to greatness is less traveled and the habits to success may be difficult for some people to sustain.

The road to success is narrow and occasionally thorny because habits that will make you successful are uncomfortable and difficult to adapt. Similar to Charles Darwin's theory of survival for the fittest, only those who manage to trim their excesses and shape their habits will eventually be successful.

Here are seven habits that will make you successful:

1. <u>Integrity</u>

Integrity is one of the measures of success. It is the ability to live an honest life free from swindling, blackmail, and corruption among other vices. Integrity is the morality of a person and is relative from one person to another. However, there is a generally accepted threshold of integrity expected of people in different social, political, and economic classes.

Integrity is uncommon to most people making it highly valuable. People will forget how you looked but will never forget how you made them feel. Integrity holds back one from committing such awful mistakes. It will help you award the deserving, condemn vices, be intolerable to corruption, and make transparency your middle name.

The lack of integrity is responsible for the downfall of great people and business empires. Political leaders worldwide have lost their crown of glory to corruption. They were once the dream of every pupil in school and aspiring young leaders looked up to them. Corruption and greed stole that from them.

So powerful is integrity that successful people guard theirs' tooth and nail. Once eroded, their success is at stake. It may crumble down like a mound hill. Do you want to be successful? Have integrity.

2. <u>An Open Mind</u>

It is the ability to tolerate and be receptive to divergent ideas different from your beliefs. It takes a lot to accommodate the opinions of others and accept their reasoning to be rational. Successful people fully understand that they do not have a monopoly on brilliant ideas. As such, they cautiously welcome the proposals of other people while allowing room for further advancement.

Entertaining the ideas of other people does not mean blindly accepting them. It is the habit of successful people to be critical of everything, balancing their options and only settling for the best. An open mind translates to an analytical and inquisitive nature. The zeal to venture into the unknown and experiment with new waters.

Successful people are distinguished from others because they challenge the status quo. They seek to improve their best and develop alternatives to the existing routines. The reason why they are successful in the first place is their open mind.

How does one have an open mind? It is by being open to infinite possibilities of a hundred and one ways of approaching issues. Routine is an enemy of open-mindedness and by extension, success. It is of course inevitable not to follow a routine at our places of work, schools, or families. It is acceptable to that extent. Being its slave is completely unacceptable.

3. Move With Time

Time is never stagnant. The world evolves around time and seasons. The wise is he who deciphers and interprets them correctly. The measure of success in these modern times is different from those in the ancient days. A lot has changed.

In this era of technological advancements, we cannot afford to live in analog ways. The poor readers of seasons are stagnant in one position for a long time. Success is elusive in their hands. A look at business giants will reveal their mastery of times and seasons. They do not fumble at it. Not one bit.

Successful businesses deal with tools of the trade of the modern world. From the great Microsoft corporation to the Coca-cola company. All of them align themselves with the market demand presently. Learning the present time and season is a habit that will elevate you to success.

4. Learn From The Mistakes of Others

It is prudent to learn from the mistakes of other people and not from yours. Keenly observe those ahead of you and watch out not to fall into their traps. It is regretful to be unable to take a cue from our predecessors and learn from their failures.

Successful people travel down roads once taken (for the advantage of hindsight) by others – except for a few adventurous ones who venture into the unknown. The benefit of hindsight is very important because we learn from the mistakes of those who preceded us and adjust accordingly. Develop a habit of watching closely those ahead of you and take a cue from them not to commit similar mistakes. This habit will propel you to the doorstep of success.

5. <u>Investment Culture</u>

It is prudent to be mindful of tomorrow. No amount of investment is too little. Successful people do not consume everything they produce. They save a portion of their income for the future. Investment is a culture developed over time. Some people find it difficult to postpone the entire consumption of their income. They will only settle when nothing is left. This is retrogressive.

An investment culture curbs wastage and emphasizes tomorrow's welfare. Moreover, to reduce risk, the investment portfolio is diversified. It is dangerous to risk everything in one endeavor. Captains of industries worldwide have invested broadly in different sectors. This makes them stay afloat even during tough economic seasons.

6. <u>Choosing Your Battles</u>

On your way to success, do not make many enemies. This habit is ancient but very relevant to date. Unnecessary fights will wear you out and divert you away from the goal. Petty distractions will hijack your focus and successfully make you unsuccessful.

Learn to train your guns on things that matter. Feed your focus and starve your fears. Ignore useless petty issues that may lead to tainting of your public image. Fight your battles wisely.

7. Learn To Listen

Listening is an art beyond hearing. It is paying detailed attention to the speech of others, both verbal and non-verbal. Always listen more and talk less – a common argument for having two ears and one mouth. To be successful, you will have to pay closer attention to what is unspoken. Listen to the way people communicate. You will pick up genuine intentions in their speech and align yourself accordingly.

Once perfected, these seven habits will make you successful.

Chapter 2:
10 Habits to Start Right Now

Have you ever wondered why you are not able to achieve your goals and aspirations? You might get a little confused while searching for the stumbling block on the way to your success, but the answer is simple and right in front of you. It is procrastination and some other unhealthy habits.

Here are ten healthy habits that you need to start incorporating in your life immediately.

1. Maintaining a Routine

You can't expect that everything will be in order one fine morning and you will start achieving all your goals suddenly just like that. It doesn't work that way. Success comes when you start taking small steps every day and slowly work on your progress little by little. You need to start to maintain a routine regularly. Doing this will help you get rid of your procrastination. You can start with simple things like doing some household chores like cooking, cleaning, etc. Let's say you have decided to cook every day – whenever you think that you need to cook all three meals and for everyone, it might intimidate you. You can start with small tasks that are more manageable. So, start with cooking an item every day. That won't take much time and won't be that difficult either – once you start doing this, start increasing the amount and intensity of the work. After you understand how this routine thing works, you can slowly move towards the work related to your goals and aspirations and maintain a routine.

2. Embracing Immediacy

Most people like to put things aside for doing those later. It is a huge mistake that can have serious consequences. People procrastinate everything like problematic things, easy things, small things, big things, and fun things. When you put aside something for doing it later, it gets more challenging to do with time. So, you just keep pushing it further and further until there is no time left to do it. You can overcome this by immediacy. Whenever you are reminded or informed about some work, start doing it immediately and don't keep it pending for later. If it is a small thing that requires a little time to finish, then make sure to finish it in one go. If it is a long work, start working immediately and take breaks and work whenever possible.

3. React Thoughtfully

Most people allow their emotions to control their reactions. Try to avoid making decisions while your emotions are heightened. This is because the decisions that are taken while emotions are heightened are usually wrong decisions and can have detrimental consequences. Your heightened emotions make you blind, and you do things that you wouldn't have done otherwise. So, whenever something triggers you, don't let your gut reaction out. Wait for some time, probably 5-6 minutes, and then act. When you give yourself a little time, it allows you to see through the situation and think beyond those overwhelming emotions. It will make you see the bigger picture and react thoughtfully.

4. Quitting Clicks, Swipes, and Scrolls

Do you even realize how much time you spend aimlessly clicking, swiping, or scrolling? It wastes a lot of your time and is also responsible for draining your productivity, concentration, and motivation. A little bit of digital media does no harm. It is, in fact, helpful because you can get loads of information from the media. But if you keep scrolling for hours, that is where the problem begins. You need to cut down on your use of media to allow yourself to get benefitted from it. If you find difficulty reducing the use of media by yourself, you can try using a browser blocker. It will block all the media outlets after a specified amount of time, thereby limiting the time you spend over there.

5. Embracing the Old

It is usual for people to crave new things every time. But sometimes, people get so overwhelmed by the excitement of trying to gain something new that they forget to cherish the things they already have in their possession. Gaining something you wanted to can be a little exciting and fun for some time, but this will just feed your urge to gain more and more things. Most people already possess everything they require, but they don't seem to see it because of the urge to get something new. For example, a person having a closet full of clothes keeps on buying new clothes every time he has somewhere to go. If you find yourself in a similar situation, you can avoid this by looking at the closet carefully and observing everything you have in your possession. You can, maybe, rearrange the closet in a way where you will be able to see stuff the way you want to see. Once you start cherishing the things that you already have, you can go a long way.

6. Remember Your Achievements

Sometimes, you are too harsh on yourself, and you blame yourself way too much. You should always treat yourself with the same amount of kindness and positivity you possess while treating others. Everyone has their fair share of successes and failures in their lives. So, you should be grateful for everything you achieved and not take those for granted. Instead of regretting and blaming yourself for the things you couldn't achieve, try reminding yourself amount the things you actually did achieve. Appreciate yourself for every good thing that you have done in your life. It can be something like quitting certain habits, scoring certain marks in an exam, doing something good for others, etc. So, whenever you make some mistake, you need to remind yourself of all the small and big things you have achieved so that you don't get too disheartened to get up and move on. Embrace the good in you!

7. Declutter

Have you ever felt that whenever you change the orientation of the furniture in your room, you get excited and feel different? This is because even a tiny change is considered to be new, fun, and exciting. Your motivation and productivity get hugely affected by your workspace environment. If your workspace environment is messy, it is going to inspire your creativity subconsciously. In contrast, if you have a well-organized workspace, it will subconsciously boost your efficiency and help you remove any mental clutter. Keep changing your workspace from time to time. Keep it messy somedays, for increasing your creativity levels. When you need to do a lot of hard work that demands efficiency, arrange everything in order and make your workspace well-organized. You can add some photo frames to give it a different and exciting look.

8. Set Small Achievable Goals Everyday

People feel the most satisfied when they know that they have achieved a certain goal. You can use it to your advantage for brightening up your day. Set small achievable goals throughout your day so that you can easily achieve them. It can be as simple as making your bed after you get up, and so on. Make sure that you already have 2-3 achieved goals before you have your breakfast. These small benchmarks play a vital role in kick-starting your day on a good note. All these little benchmarks add up and give you a sense of pride and satisfaction after you achieve them, thereby brightening up your day.

9. Give Compliments

People love to receive compliments from others but get a little shaky while giving compliments to others. Have you ever wondered why? It is probably because you worry about how it would make you look like. You feel that complimenting others can make you look lighter and easy. That's absolutely not the case. Complimenting people can really help you start a conversation with different people and get friendly. It is a fantastic social skill that you need to learn because of the various benefits it offers. Don't fear what others will think, and don't sugarcoat your words either. Because when you give fake compliments, people can feel that it is not coming from your heart, leaving a very negative impression on them. Try to be as genuine as possible and speak your mind out.

10. Commit to Relaxation

A lot of people work continuously, and even when they are taking a break, all they think about is their work! It is not a healthy habit and needs to be changed immediately. When you work yourself too much and don't give yourself the amount of relaxation it deserves, work seems to be more complicated than it actually is, thereby reducing your productivity and concentration. When you feel like you can't work anymore and that you have reached your threshold cut yourself some slack! When you are taking a break, make sure not to think about work at all. Plan something relaxing, exciting, or fun, and enjoy yourself fully while taking some time off from your work. It will recharge your mind, and then you can return to your work, being energetic and positive.

I hope you follow these steps and develop them as habits in your daily life so that you can make the most out of your life and stay happy.

Chapter 3:
10 Habits to Change Your Life

I'm sure everyone wonders at a certain point in their life that what is the thing that is stopping them from reaching their goals. It is your bad and unhealthy habits that hold you down. If you want to succeed in life, you need to get rid of these habits and adopt healthy habits to help you in the long run.

Here are 10 healthy habits that will change your life completely if you can adopt them in your daily life:

1. Start Following a Morning Ritual

Everyone has something that they love to do, i.e., things that boost their energy and uplifts their mood. Find one for yourself and do that every morning. It will help you kickstart your day with a bright and cheerful mood. It will also help you to eliminate mental fatigue and stress. You will find yourself super energetic and productive. Let me tell you some morning rituals that you can try and get benefitted from.

- *Eating Healthy:* If you are very passionate about health and fitness, eating healthy as a morning ritual might be a win-win situation for you. You can have a nutritious breakfast every morning. Balance your breakfast with proper amounts of carbs, fats, proteins, etc. It will not only help you in staying healthy but will also help you kickstart your day on a proactive note.

- *Meditating:* Meditation is an excellent way of clearing your mind, enhancing your awareness, and improving your focus. You can meditate for 20 to 30 minutes every morning. Then you can take a nice warm shower, followed by a fresh cup of coffee. Most importantly, meditating regularly will also help you strengthen your immune system, promote emotional stability, and reduce stress.

- *Motivating:* A daily dose of motivation can work wonders for you. When you are motivated, your productivity doubles, and you make the best out of your day. Every morning, you can simply ask yourself questions like, "If it is the last day of your life, what do you want to do?", "What productive thing can I do today to make the best out of the day" "What do I need to do in order to avoid regretting later for having wasted a day?". When you ask yourself questions like these, you are actually instructing your brain to be prepared for having a packed-up and productive day.

- *Writing:* Writing can be a super-effective way of kickstarting your day. When you journal all your thoughts and emotions every day after waking up, it allows you to relieve yourself from all the mental clutter, unlocks your creative side, and sharpens your focus.

- *Working Out:* Working out is a great morning ritual that you can follow every day. When you work out daily, it helps you burn more fat, improves your blood circulation, and boosts your energy level. If you are interested in fitness and health, this is the perfect morning ritual for you. You can do some cardio exercises, or some strength training, or both. Depending on your suitability, create a workout routine for yourself and make sure to stick to that. If you don't stick to your routine, it won't be of much help.

2. Start Following the 80/20 Rule

The 80/20 rule states that almost 20% of the tasks you perform are responsible for yielding 80% of the results. It is why you should invest more time in tasks that can give you more significant results instead of wasting your time on tasks that yield little to no results. In this way, you can not only save time but also maximize your productivity. Most importantly, when you see the results after performing those tasks, you will be more motivated to complete the following tasks. After you have finished performing these tasks, now you can quickly move your concentration and focus towards other activities that you need to do throughout your day.

3. Practice Lots of Reading

Reading is a great habit and a great way to stimulate your creativity and gaining more knowledge. When you get immersed in reading, it calms you and improves your focus, almost similar to meditating. If you practice reading before going to bed, you are going to have a fantastic sleep. You can read non-fiction books, which will help you seek motivation, develop new ideas, and broaden your horizon. You can also get a lot of advice about how to handle certain situations in life.

4. Start Single-tasking

Multitasking is hard, and almost 2% of the world's total population can do this properly. You can try multitasking occasionally. If you keep on trying to do this all the time, it will form a mental clutter, and as a result, your brain won't be able to filter out unnecessary information. Many studies have suggested that it can severely damage your cognitive control and lower your efficiency when you multitask a lot. It is the main reason why you should try to do single-tasking more than multitasking. Prepare a list of all the tasks you need to perform in a day and start with the most important one. Make sure not to rush and to complete one thing at a time.

5. Start Appreciating More

Appreciating things is totally dependent on your mentality. For example, some people can whine and complain about a glass being half empty, whereas some people appreciate that there is half a glass of water. It totally depends on your point of view and way of thinking. People get blinded by the urge to reach success so much that they actually forget to appreciate the little things in life. If you are working and earning a handsome salary, don't just sit and complain about why you are not earning more, what you need to do to achieve that, etc. You should obviously aim high, but not at the cost of your well-being. When you practice gratitude, it increases your creativity, improves your physical health, and reduces your stress. You can start writing about the things you are grateful for in your journal every day before going to bed, make some time for appreciating your loved ones, or remind yourself of all the things you are grateful for before going to bed every day. If you are not happy with your current situation, you will not be happy in the future. You need to be happy and satisfied at first, and then only you can work on progressing further.

6. Always Keep Positive People Around You

When you have toxic people around you, it gets tough for you to stay in a good mood or achieve something good in life. Toxic people always find a way to pull you down and make you feel bad about yourself. You should always surround yourself with people who are encouraging and positive. When you do that, your life is going to be full of positivity.

7. Exercise on a Regular Basis

Start exercising regularly to maintain good health and enhancing your creativity and cognitive skills. It also increases your endurance level and boosts your energy. When you exercise regularly, your body produces more endorphins. These hormones work as anti-depressants.

8. Start Listening More

Effective communication is very important in maintaining both professional and personal relationships. For communicating effectively, you need to work on your listening capability first. You need to pay attention to the things said by others instead of focusing only on what you have to say. Listening to others will allow you to understand them better. When you listen to someone, it makes them understand that they are valued and that you are here to listen to them. When they feel important and valued, they also start paying attention to what you say, thereby contributing to effective communication. Don't try to show fake concentration while you are busy thinking about something else. When you listen more, you learn more.

9. Take a Break from Social Media (Social Media Detox)

Many studies have shown that excessive use of social media can contribute to depression. Most importantly, it wastes a lot of time because people meaninglessly scroll, swipe, and click for hours. It is a very unhealthy habit and is very bad for bothe physical and mental health. Sometimes you need to completely stop using social media for a while to reduce mental clutter and stress. Turn off your laptops and phones every day for a few hours. It will help you to reconnect with the surrounding world and will uplift your mood.

10. Start Investing More in Self-care

Make some time for yourself out of your busy schedule. It is going to boost your self-esteem, improve your mental health, and uplift your mood. You need to do at least one thing for yourself every day that will make you feel pampered and happy. You can prepare a mouth-watering meal, take a comfortable bubble bath, learn something new, or just relax while listening to music.

The moment you start introducing these habits in your daily, you will instantly see change. Remember that even a tiny step towards a positive change can give outstanding results if you stay consistent.

Chapter 4:
10 Habits of Warren Buffet

Warren Buffett, popularly known as the "Oracle of Omaha", is the chairman and CEO of Berkshire Hathaway and an American investor, corporate magnate, and philanthropist. He's undoubtedly a well-known investor of all time-if, not history, continuously setting records of knowledge, talent, and a strong drive to reach his future objectives. Buffett is also a supporter of leadership and personal growth, and he shares his wealth of advice to help you better your decisions.

So, how did he land to success? Here are ten warren's habits, which would you benefits later on.

1. **His Reading Habit**

Reading- a habit that he adheres to religiously, is one rule that Warren Buffett considers key to success. So he reads The Wall Street Journal, USA Today, and Forbes in the mornings and The Financial Times, The New York Times, Omaha World-Herald, and American Banker throughout the day.

Reading is basic to improving your understanding. Among other books, self-improvement books are popular with Buffet. That's said, consider jogging your memory with a mind-stimulating activity like reading. Engage in "500" pages book, article, newspaper each day, in the area that self-improves your interests. Reading makes you more knowledgeable than other people.

2. **Compound Your Life and Finances**

As per Albert Einstein, "Compound interest is the world's eighth wonder." if you understand it, you earn it; if not, you pay it." Warren Buffet's approach to investments never changes. He maintains his compounding investment principle as an investing strategy and aligns it with thinking patterns.

Compounding is the practice of reinvesting your earnings in your principal to generate an exponential return. Are you compounding your life finances, relationships, reading? That is how knowledge operates. It accumulates in the same way that compound interest does. You can accomplish it, but best when you're determined!

3. **Isolation Power**

Despite becoming the world's best investor and stock market trader, Warren Buffett claims that living away from Wall Street helped him. When you block the outside influence, you think quickly, distract unimportant variables and the general din.

Isolation exposes you to more prospects as it keeps you from external influence and information, making you unique and infamous.

4. Managing Your Time Wisely

You'll have 24 hours a day, or 1,440 minutes. All the leaders and successful people like Warren have one thing in common because of how powerful it is: Time management.

5. Do What You Enjoy

Your career or business may start with low returns but approaching it in Warren's way means switching your mind entirely to the job. If your mind likes something and you feed it to it regularly, it never turns off.

Working for a low salary is a momentary inconvenience, but it multiplies at the rate your skills increases, and they grow tremendously because you enjoy doing it.

6. Inner and Outer Scorecards

The key question about how people act is whether they have an Internal or an outward scorecard. So, naturally, it is preferable to be happy with your Inner Score to live a peaceful and happy life.

Having an inner scorecard is being contented with your thoughts and making decisions based on those thoughts while ignoring external influences or judgement skills. The deal is to live through values that matter to you, especially when making tough financial decisions.

7. Mimic the Finest Managers' Leadership Behaviours

Much of your life endeavours are, in most cases, shaped by the person who you choose to admire and emulate. Warren's admiration of Tom Murphy scourged him to greatness in leading his businesses to success.

8. Understand What You Have

Know and understand the companies in which you have a stake. Examine and analyze what is going on within the company, not what is going on in the marketplace.

The company's operations should be straightforward such that you can explain to an 8-year-old child how the company produces money in one phase. Familiarize enough with your investments while keeping a tab with its exact worth.

9. Invest in Your Well-Being

The basic right towards success is your well-being. Take care of your mental and physical health first, especially when you're young. The importance of life's fundamentals- nutritious diet, regular exercise, and restful sleep-is self-evident. It all boils down to whether you're doing them correctly.

10. Create a Positive Reputation

Buffett's reputation stems from his moral and level-headed attitude to both his personal and business life. You should view your business/career as a reflection of yourself, which means you should be careful and sensitive of how your decisions influence others.

Conclusion

Just as Warren, enhance your cognitive skills through learning to become more knowledgeable for bettering your life initiatives. While focusing on your major goals, take care of your mental and physical well-being. Therefore, invest your efforts and time carefully because the returns will multiply eventually.

Chapter 5:
7 Habits To Change Your Life

Consistently, habit drives you to do what you do—regardless of whether it's a matter of considerations or conduct that happens naturally. Whatever that is, imagine a scenario where you could saddle the power of your habits to improve things. Envision a day to day existence where you have a habit for finishing projects, eating admirably, staying in contact with loved ones, and working to your fullest potential. At the point when you have an establishment of beneficial routines, you're setting yourself up for a full, sound, and effective life.

Here are 7 habits that Can change your entire life.

1. Pinpoint and Focus Entirely on Your K eystone Routine

Charles Duhigg, in his power book stipulates the essence of recognizing your Keystone Habit—the habit you distinguish as the main thing you can change about your life. To discover what that is for you, ask yourself, what continually worries you? Is it something you would that you like to stop, or something you would do and prefer not to begin? The cornerstone habit is distinctive for everybody, and it might take a couple of meetings of profound thought to pinpoint precisely what that habit is. Whichever propensity you're chipping away at, pick each in turn. More than each in turn will be overpowering and will improve your probability of neglecting to improve any habits. Be that as it may, don't really accept that you can just change one thing about yourself; it's really the inverse. Dealing with this one Keystone Habit can have a positive gradually expanding influence into the remainder of your life also.

2. Recognize Your Present Daily Practice and the Reward You Get From It.

Suppose you need to fabricate a habit for getting to the workplace a half hour early every day. You need to do this since you figured the extra peaceful time in the morning hours will assist you with being more gainful, and that profitability will be compensated by an expanded feeling of occupation fulfilment, and a generally speaking better workplace. As of now, you get to the workplace simply on schedule. Your present routine is to take off from your home in a hurry, at the specific time you've determined that (without traffic or episode) will get you to chip away at time. Your award is investing some additional energy at your home in the first part of the day, spending an additional half hour dozing or "charging your batteries" for the day ahead.

3. Take the Challenges Into Consideration.

Challenges are regularly prompts that push you to fall once more into old habits. In the case of having to get to work earlier, your challenges may lie in your rest designs the prior night, or in organizing plans with a partner. These difficulties won't mysteriously vanish so you need to consider them. In any case, don't let the presence of challenges, or stress that new difficulties will come up later on, discourage you from setting up your new propensities. In the event that your difficulties incorporate planning with others, make them a piece of your new daily practice, as I'll clarify later. At this moment, basically recognize what the difficulties or obstructions are.

4. Plan and Identifying Your New Routine

Old habits never vanish; they are basically supplanted with new propensities. In the case of getting to the workplace earlier, the new standard includes going out a half hour sooner. On the off chance that the old habit was remunerated with the possibility that you'll have more energy for the day by remaining in your home longer, the new propensity needs to centre around the possibility that more rest doesn't really mean more energy. All in all, you'll need to address what you think you'll be surrendering by supplanting the old habit.

5. Reinforce a 30 Days Challenge.

By and large, your inability to minister beneficial routines basically comes from not adhering to them. A lot of studies show that habits, when performed day by day, can turn out to be important for your daily schedule in just 21 days. So set a beginning date and dispatch your game plan for a preliminary 30-day time span.

6. Empower Your Energy Through Setbacks.

Here and there, it's not simply self-control that runs out. Now and then you are influenced from your ways by life "hindering" new objectives. In the event that something influences you from your test, the best game-plan is to assess the circumstance and perceive how you can get around, finished, or through that deterrent. Notwithstanding, when another propensity is set up, it really turns into our default setting. Assuming your standard habits are sound, unpleasant occasions are less inclined to lose you from your typical schedules. All in all, we're similarly prone to default to solid habits as we are to self-undermining habits, if those sound habits have become a piece of our ordinary daily practice.

7. Account Yourself and for Your Actions Publicly (Hold Yourself Accountable).

Your encouraging people are the most significant asset you will have at any point. Regardless of whether it's your closest companion, your accomplice or your Facebook posts, being responsible to somebody other than yourself will help you adhere to your objective. Simply remember that "responsible" isn't equivalent to "declaration". Anybody can advise the world they will rise ahead of schedule from here on out. However, on the off chance that that individual has a group of allies behind them, whom they routinely update, they are bound to stay with their new propensity during times when they are building up their new habit and inspiration is coming up short.

Chapter 6:
10 Habits of Unsuccessful People

Highly successful people (in any of the many ways that "success" can be defined) seem to recognize a few basic principles. The most important of these is that your energy, not your time, is restricted each day and must be carefully controlled.

Here are 10 of the most popular self-imposed blocks that have a troll on your success. If you come across one, use it as a cue to reevaluate, reflect, and change direction.

1. Worry of the Most Unlikely Outcome.

Despite its label as a "maladaptive trait," worrying has an evolutionary connection to intelligence. This is why, according to Jeremy Coplan, lead author of a study published of Frontiers in Evolutionary Neuroscience, effective people are naturally nervous.

Whatever the case may be, to work correctly, you must be able to distinguish between which fears are worth reacting to and which are your brain's attempt to "prepare" you for survival by conjuring up the most severe possible risk. This is an antiquated, animalistic mechanism that is useless in everyday life. Highly effective people should not spend their time worrying about the things that are least likely to happen.

2. Just Talking the Talk.

"I'm preparing to do this and that." What's better than announcing on social media that you're starting a business? Putting it into action.

Entrepreneur Derek Sivers argued in his 2010 TED talk, "Keep Your Goals to Yourself," that disclosing your intentions can be detrimental rather than inspiring. People will sometimes applaud you just for stating your purpose, he said, and this applause, ironically, may drain your motivation to carry out the plans you've just outlined.

"Psychotherapists have discovered that telling others your goal and having them embrace it is known as a 'social reality,'" Sivers explained in his talk. "The mind is deceived into believing it has already been accomplished. Then, after you've had your satisfaction, you're less likely to put in the necessary effort."

There's nothing wrong with expressing your happiness. However, try to keep your mouth shut before you have good news, not just good intentions.

3. Ruminating and Not Doing Anything About It.

Reflecting becomes ruminating as the intention to act dissolves in favor of constantly replaying certain situations or issues through your mind.

Self-awareness is common among highly successful individuals, or at least it should be. This means they devote a significant amount of time to reflecting on their behavior and experiences and determining how they can change. However, they do not waste mental energy pondering what went wrong rather than consciously modifying what needs to be changed to fix the issue.

4. Choosing the Wrong People To Spend Time With.

The people you hang out with can either inspire you to be your best self or bring out your worst traits. Spend time with people who can motivate you to make the changes you want to make in your life. Do you want to fail at that goal completely? If it's the case, spend time with people who gloat about their bad habits. People get their energy from each other. Always remember that you are the average of the 5 people that you spend most of your time with.

5. Being Resentful for Taking Time for Themselves.

People who have experienced any degree of success understand that it is a multi-faceted operation. You won't be able to work at your best if you're tired, undernourished, or experiencing some other sort of extreme imbalance in your life.

As a result, highly successful individuals are just as dedicated to relaxation and health as work and efficiency. They don't stress themselves up about how much they should have done in a three-day weekend or why they shouldn't take time off when they need it.

6. Constantly Concentrating on the Negative.

It's mind-boggling to focus on the negative aspects of life because it'll only make you feel worse. You don't have to believe that life is simple to concentrate on the positive. You should maintain a rational viewpoint without always pointing out the flaws in everything you see.

We've all met someone who is still complaining about something. "Ugh, it rained this morning, and my shoes were soaked through and through." Yes, that's a disappointment. You won't be able to affect the weather, unfortunately. You should put on a new pair of shoes if you want to.

It's fine if you're having a rough day; we're all irritable at times; everybody gets irritable now and then. However, you are living a poor life if you despise anything. That's what there is to it.

7. Justifying Their Place in Life.

Taking on exceptional work also elicits questions and, at times, judgments from those who don't believe in your project or are suspicious of its long-term viability. Constantly feeling the need to explain or justify your role in life, on the other hand, is not only exhausting but also unnecessary. Highly effective people understand that you can't get approval from people who don't want it.

8. Allowing Themselves To Be Sucked Into a State of Laziness.

We've all had times when we've been compelled to cancel plans. Leaving the house, even for something "fun," can feel like a Herculean task at times.

However, it is fresh and novel experiences that make life so beautiful. You aren't fully involved in your own life when you succumb to laziness, which is unfair to your friends, family, spouse, and those who want to share it with you.

9. Worrying That Isn't Essential and Unregulated Thought Patterns.

Worrying is among the most common ways people drain their energy doing. It is the act of anticipating the worst-case scenario and assuming that it is not only probable but most likely.

Worrying does not make you more equipped to deal with life's challenges instead, it makes you more likely to build your fears. You'd be surprised to learn that 99.9% of your worries were baseless and never "came true" if you made a list of everything you've ever worried about in your life.

If you just made a list of everything you didn't care about in life, you'd find that worrying didn't change anything; it just sapped your energy at the moment. The only thing it has done for you is that it made things more complicated, twisted, and less fun. It is not only ineffective, but completely pointless as well. Highly successful people learn to concentrate on something else rather than spend their time worrying about what could go wrong.

10. There Is Just Too Much Optimistic Thought.

It's self-evident that no one achieves remarkable success without first confronting destructive thought patterns. What's less evident is that highly successful people don't partake in excessive positive thinking, which can be arbitrary, distorted, and even distracting in excess. Worse, they set themselves up for failure or disappointment by thinking too positively. Instead, highly successful people understand the power of neutral thought, which means they don't try to make life into something.

Conclusion

If you don't want to be an unsuccessful person, you need to make a conscious effort to avoid doing these things. Focus on the habits that would bring you positive change instead, which we will discuss in another segment.

Chapter 7:
6 Reasons your emotions are getting in the way of your success

Do you ever ponder on why your new year's resolutions fail miserably? It is primarily because of the toxic emotions and our negative thoughts of the past that keeps us stuck with the same patterns and regrets. We can try to change and manage our attitudes well, but the emotions are out of our hands. So even though we can't control what we feel, we must confront them to achieve our goals and resolutions.

A therapist in Tarzana, California, Vicki Botnick, explains that any emotion – even elation, joy, or others you would typically view as positive – can intensify to a point where it becomes difficult to control.

Here are 6 Reasons why emotions are getting in the way of your success

1. You let your emotions rule you

Most of us are clueless about taking control of our emotions and how they affect our productivity. But we must manage them if we strive to achieve our goals. Emotions are an instant response to a specific trigger. All of our emotions are interlinked with each other. For example, we can't taste the satisfaction of joy if we don't go through any pain, or we can't enjoy courage without being fearful first. All of these emotions are what make us human. Embracing both negative and positive emotions are essential, but if they start to get in the way of your success, then you must take action and act upon them.

2. Anger.

"The greatest remedy for anger is a delay." - Thomas Paine.

Anger is the majorly common emotion that humankind feels. This negative emotion can result from frustrations, conflicts, mistreatment, or interpersonal conflicts, or is sometimes triggered by an event or experience that happened in the past. For example, suppose you studied really hard for a test but didn't get the expected grade. The next time when you're willing to give it another try, you won't study as much as you did the first time because you'll remember your previous failed attempt. You will re-live your failure and will eventually become frustrated and demotivated. The best thing to do in this scenario is just to take some time off and breathe. Distance yourself from everything and get yourself to calm down before making any decision. Ask yourself then, are you too hard on yourself? Are you trying to do everything at once that's causing you to get upset? Have you set the bar too high? Ponder on these questions and then look for the solutions calmly. Being angry about the things you can't control is pointless, as anger feeds more anger, and you would get stuck in an endless loop of resentment and frustration. Seek solutions on the things you can control and be patient.

3. Fear.

The fear of failure is perhaps the worst emotion we can endure. It snatches away even the slightest chance of taking that first step to achieving our dreams and goals. The reasons why we are so afraid of failures may vary from person to person. Some people can't digest that they are full of flaws and that failure is the most crucial step towards leading a successful life. They want to win no matter what. Others might feel that they are not good enough if they can't achieve something. Most people don't admit that they have fears. Fear can either be your greatest friend or your worst enemy; it all depends on how you treat it, whether you look into its eyes and face it or run from it. Living fearlessly doesn't mean that a person isn't afraid of anything, but rather that the person has befriended his fears and is now dancing with them. One shouldn't run away from the challenges that the world throws at him, but stand up to them bravely and face them. Make a list of all the things that scare you or are distracting you from achieving your goals. And then work towards them until they no longer bother you or gets in the way of your success. A famous African proverb states, "Smooth seas do not make skillful sailors."

4. **Envy.**

Bertrand Russell once said, "Beggars do not envy millionaires, though of course, they will envy other beggars who are more successful." Envy and jealousy are the two strongest emotions that mankind has experienced. Although they go hand in hand with each other, there is still a slight difference between them. Being envious wants the other person's things, while jealousy wants the other person's recognition from others. Whenever things tend to go south, we start to become envious of those who are successful. We compare ourselves to them, idealize their successes, and in the process, we lose ourselves. We shift our focus from our signs of progress to being demotivated and stressed out. Pain is an indicator of progress. When we stretch our minds beyond our comfort zone, we feel pain. This pain is the indication that we should move forward and not run away. We shouldn't compare our initial progress to those who have been striving for years. Everyone has their own pace. We should focus on ourselves and setting our potentials free.

5. **Guilt.**

The guilt of doing something else or saying something else instead of what you already did or said will forever haunt us. Guilt gets us stuck in the past rather than live in the present moment. There is a term in psychology, The Zeigarnik Effect, which refers that people remember uncompleted tasks more than the completed ones. They then blame themselves for not doing it sooner or better. Our mindset is often linked with productivity blame, where we feel bad for achieving something or not working hard enough. We tend to punish ourselves emotionally and get the idea that we can never reach our goals. But it is essential to take some time off and treat yourself with kindness and empathy. Don't over-pressurize yourself. Self-appreciate and become a better version of yourself in the process. "Mistakes are always forgivable if one dares to admit them." - Bruce Lee.

6. **Sadness.**

"We must understand that sadness is an ocean, and sometimes we drown, while other days, we are forced to swim." - R.M. Drake.

Feeling sad or low on energy crushes productivity and enthusiasm. We feel demotivated and can't focus on our tasks. Sadness makes us feel secluded and isolated. We must embrace this emotion at our own pace, but we shouldn't hide away from whatever it is that's bothering us. Start again slowly with your productivity, make slight progress, start rechallenging yourself. But don't do all of this unless you feel okay again.

Conclusion:

Understanding how your emotions are getting in the way of your productivity requires practice. Self-awareness is the key to know yourself better, so you can deal with your emotions efficiently. Please pay close attention to what your feelings are trying to tell you rather than running away from them.

Chapter 8:
10 Habits of Jeff Bezos

As you know, your lifestyle choices can make or break your success. It began in a basement and has since grown into a well-known online shopping app. Jeff Bezos' brainchild, the "Everything Store," is a platform where people get online deals. Commonly known as Amazon.com, the "Everything Store" is billion dollars' worth.

Jeff Bezos' habits vary from what to read to dealing with stress, which he phrases as "laugh a lot." Bezos, the self-made millionaire and Amazon CEO, is one of the world's wealthiest persons. But, what got him there? His natural aptitude for business got him there. Moreover, his habits are key to his achievements.

Here are ten business-oriented Jeff Bezos' habits for innovative-minds upkeep.

1. Customer-Centric Approach

Unlike most of the business, Bezos and Amazon have in decades ignored a "profitable" approach to doing business; instead, he invests in a customer-centric approach. Although at some point Amazon got chastised by publishers for allowing the laity to evaluate books, Amazon encouraged its consumers to share their comments, whether critical or negative.

An incentive that created a Clientele review platform which is why Amazon.com is today's most trusted e-commerce platform. Keeping a soundtrack of your customers means that you're taking good care of them.

2. Make Your Plan Based on Things That Will Not Change

While trading your brands-be it, lipstick, tractor seats, e-book readers, or data storages, make bigger plans with these constants: Provider your clientele with a broader selection scope, lower pricing, and rapid, dependable delivery.

3. Create Your Own Rules

If you despise writing essays, Amazon might not be the place for you. Amazon made it a rule early that anyone who wishes to suggest a new concept must first condense their views into a six-page booklet.

Before making any decisions, everyone concerned, must read and analyze the six-pager. And also, according to Bezos, "no team should be so large that two pizzas won't be enough." When your organization is far larger to be fed by two pizzas, divide it into fewer independent units of your own liking and capabilities to compete for limited resources while making your customers happy.

4. Work Backwards to What Your Customers Require

Customers' desires, rather than drivers' preferences, have shaped the specifications for Amazon's significant new projects, such as the Kindle tablets and e-book readers. So if your clientele doesn't want something, let it go, even if it means dismantling a once-powerful department.

5. Master the Art of Failure

Bezos's Amazon recruited many editors to produce book and music evaluations but later decided to use user feedback instead. A move that failed miserably.

Such blunders, according to Bezos, are a normal part of your innovative life, as long as you're on a learning reality, failure is sometimes positive. To succeed as an innovator, means that you are in for such flaws as taking risks, failing at a point while tucking your sleeves for a changes.

6. Make Informed Choices or Decisions

If you did know that Amazon began as a bookstore, well, here you have it! Bezos' product decisions are always a product of well thought logics and factual data rather than incidental incentives. Your product decision should be knowledgeable, and reading is knowledge.

In a nutshell, books are the ideal driver for e-commerce. Because nearly every aspect of commerce and customer behavior can be quantified, and almost all choices are based on data. Meetings are about metrics, not tales from customers!

7. You Are Willing To Be Misinterpreted for a Long Time

Many of Bezos-Amazon's initiatives appear as money-losing distractions. Which severally send the company's stock price down and earns the wrath of focal analysts. A five-to-seven-year financial plan is acceptable if your new initiatives make strategic sense to you.

8. Don't Mind the Competition

If your business is imitating and engrossed in what others are doing, then you're off Jeff Bezos' innovative strategies. In truth, client service should always come first. Just as Amazon Prime, succeed in your innovative plans while satisfying your clientele-base.

9. Don't Try To Be a Blockbuster

Your present success does not guarantee your future relevance. Consider the fate of Blockbuster Video and accept the fact that your industry advances with time, and will never hold similar standing as of now. Pay close attention to evolving state of affairs as you lead the change rather than reacting to it.

10. Ditch Complexity

Startups are characterized by rapid decision-making and innovation. However, as a company grows, it is frequently delayed by complexity. This suffocates innovation. Just like Bezos, always treat your company as a start-up at the cutting edge.

Conclusion

Following Jeff Bezos uniqueness will not guarantee you $100 billion. But you'll still set yourself up for a more prosperous future with your company endeavors if you maintain this proactive, forward-thinking approach.

PART 2

Chapter 1:
7 Habits That Are Good For You

The cognitive ability to distinguish what is good from what is bad for us is an invaluable skill. Cherry-picking nutritive habits in a world full of all manner of indecency comes handy especially if you want to stand out from the crowd.

Here are 7 habits that are good for you:

1. <u>Waking Up Early</u>

The early bird catches the worm. Early risers have the opportunity to pick the best for themselves before the rest of the world is awake. It is healthy and prudent to wake up early and start your day before most people do. You leverage on opening your business early before your competitors. Besides, the preparedness of early risers is unmatched even as the day progresses.

Waking up early is not a reserve for 'busy people' only. It is for everyone in this world of survival for the fittest. We all have 24 hours in one day. The difference comes from how we use our time. One may spend more than 8 hours sleeping and another will spend just 6 hours for the same. You cannot sleep as if you are competing with the dead and expect to make it in the land of the living.

Early risers are active people. They are as alert as chamois, prepared for any eventuality.

2. Associate With Successful People

Show me your friends and I will show you what kind of person you are. Success, like most things, is contagious. In his book *48 laws of power*, Robert Greene writes *'avoid the unhappy and unlucky.'* This is not discrimination. Association with the unhappy and unlucky will contaminate you with negative energy.

Associate with successful people and you will follow their example. You will emulate their saving culture, their investment behavior, and their aggressiveness in business. In the shadow of the successful, you will attract positivity and grow exponentially. Maintain knit relationships with the successful.

3. Be Teachable

A teachable spirit will take you places where your character will not. A teachable person is capable of receiving correction graciously without perceiving it as demeaning. Do not be afraid of getting things wrong. Instead, be worried when you lack the humility to accept correction.

Being teachable is one of the greatest strengths you can have. We all are a work in progress, never finished products. What happens when you refuse to be under the tutelage of the successful and experienced? The greatest lessons are not learned in a classroom but the school of life.

4. Accepting Challenges

When challenged by circumstances we face, be the bigger brother/sister. Take challenges positively and work towards a solution instead of whining about this or that. Our patience, skills, and competence are sometimes put to the test. A test so subtle that we fail without even realizing it. When you have a positive mindset of accepting challenges, you will ace the game. Prove your worth wherever you are through your actions, never by your words.

When you accept a challenge and conquer it, it takes you to another level. The beauty of life lies in progress with the assurance that change is a constant. Accept challenges towards positivity and not the dark ones. Ignore that which derails your purpose or goes against your principles.

5. <u>Learn When To Retreat and To Advance</u>

The art of knowing when to push or pull is important in life. On the battlefield, retreating and advancing by troops is a call their leader makes. He decides that for his team based on his training, the immediate situation, and his judgment. Retreating is not a sign of weakness; neither is advancing a sign of strength. Both are strategies to win a war.

It is okay to retreat from a cause you were pursuing or to adjust your plans. Just make it worth your while. When you resume, be stronger than before. Again, when you retreat, do not succumb to the ridicule of your enemies when they mistake it for weakness. The fear of what the opinion of others (non-entities) is should not make you afraid of retreating to strategize.

When you make up your mind to advance with a noble course, advance skillfully. Do not advance blindly or ignorant of what you intend to achieve. Train your focus on the target.

6. <u>Ask for help.</u>

We are mortals; facing deficiencies here and there. We do not always have the answer to everything. Ask for help from the knowledgeable ones when in a quagmire.

Asking for help is not a weakness. It is appreciating the strengths of others. It is also appreciating the diversity of the human race that we are not endowed with everything. The silent rule is that you should be careful whom you approach for help. Some ill-intentioned people will sink you deep into trouble.

Nevertheless, asking for help is perfectly normal and it is something you should try sometimes. When you ask for help from the experienced, you save yourself the trouble of making messy mistakes. Learn through others who trod down the same road. Their lessons are invaluable; you will avoid their mistakes.

7. <u>Develop hobbies.</u>

Hobbies are those things you engage in for fun. They are very important because you take a break from your daily hustles. In your hobbies, you are carefree. You do not have to worry about your boss or business partners.

Hobbies are meant to be fun. If you are not having fun when doing your hobbies, probably they are no longer one. You should consider finding new ones. All work without play makes Jack a dull boy.

Hobbies are good for you. Go for swimming or that road trip, find a sport and play for fun, go beyond singing in the shower, travel everywhere you desire, or even start watching that TV series you are always curious about. Variety is the spice of life. Do not be afraid to spice up your life with all that your heart desires.

The above 7 habits are good for you. They will help you grow and increase your productivity in all you do.

Chapter 2:
6 Habits of Oprah Winfrey

When anyone utters the name "Oprah Winfrey," one of her most iconic quotes comes to mind: "You get a car, and everyone else gets a car." While most business people applaud the "to-do roster," Oprah is not one of them; instead, she values meditation, no alarms, and limiting business operations to the necessary minimum. From a poor rural Mississippi upbringing to getting a full scholarship and to landing a seat on the morning talk program, Baltimore Is Talking, to now solidifying her reputation as a global legend and America's first black billionaire, with a net worth of US$2.5 billion, you might be wondering – exactly how she does it?

Oprah Winfrey maintains a series of daily routines-from getting up early to work out to practicing Gratitude. This daily routine, as she notes, keeps her happy, grounded, and humble.

Here are six daily habits from the legend herself that you might want to make your own.

1. **Her Day Starts With Morning Rituals.**

Oprah Winfrey starts her mornings with a sequence of spiritual exercises, allowing her body to wake up and her mind to focus on Gratitude and self-reflection. She meditates for approximately 20 minutes. If the weather is nice, she sits in her lawn chair with her eyes closed, simply reminiscing on the previous day and imagining her aspirations for the day ahead. She noted that starting the day slowly allows her mind to wake up and become entirely focused on the day ahead.

2. Working Out Every Morning.

Oprah's journey to weight loss has been a struggle over the years. She opened up on her efforts with maintaining a healthy weight and fitness program. She highlighted in an interview that she loves sweating it up through the regular old-fashioned cardio exercises, explicitly on an elliptical machine followed by a treadmill. She then follows with some regular bodyweight training before warming up for some sit-ups.

Although there is ongoing research on whether a better fitness routine should be in the morning or the evening, substantial studies describe several morning fitness benefits. To mention a few, You'll eat fewer calories; you'll have more energy throughout the day, burn more bothersome fat cells, and sleep better when the sun goes down.

3. She Consumes a Lot of Vegetables.

If you don't pay attention when your mother or your partner softly encourages you to eat more of Mother Earth's natural creations, maybe you'll listen to Oprah Winfrey.

Oprah confessed in an interview that she values her lunch more than any other meal, and one of her meals go-to involves a big, overflowing salad of green goodness. She noted that the salad is usually from the veggies from her home garden. As she put its's "as a rule, if we can grow it, we don't buy it."

You probably don't need us to tell you that veggies are excellent for your diet. Still, science backs up Winfrey's meal plan, as a well-balanced, vegetable patch diet can help fight cancer, heart disease, diabetes, and hypertension, among other conditions.

4. Oprah Schedules Time To Unwind.

There's no doubt that Winfrey's itinerary would be overwhelming for most people, with regular meetings, phone conversations, and traveling, but achieving this degree of esteem necessitates astute management and perseverance. However, if you look into the lives of individuals at the pinnacle of success, such as Winfrey, you'll notice that they constantly make time to unwind.

In an interview about her daily life, Winfrey stated that she relaxes before retiring to bed by reading frequently. Though you may not have Winfrey's gorgeous fireplace to warm you up as you flip the pages over, the research found that individuals who read before bed are less anxious than those who watch Netflix.

5. Practicing Gratitude daily.

The benefits of practicing Gratitude have been proven for centuries, even though gestures to the same have become popular recently. Oprah maintains with her volumes of gratitude diaries that she usually jots down before going to bed. She makes a list of things that have given her tremendous joy or which she is grateful for.

Implementing this habit will not only improve your health but also increase your empathy and self-confidence. One study suggests that thinking about what you're thankful for rather than contemplating on the to-do list each night helps better your sleep.

6. She Manages Her Finances.

You'd think someone of Winfrey's caliber would employ someone to manage her finances, but while she got a whole team, she oversees the minutiae of her fortune daily. She claims that she cannot delegate all financial decisions to others because she had a poor upbringing and prefers to understand what comes in and what goes out of her earnings.

She noted during an interview that it is crucial for her to personally manage her finances as doing so relieves her from surprises of what she has and doesn't have.

While most of us struggle with the very thought about money, research has shown that the more you train yourself to handle your finances, the better your chances of becoming wealthy.

Conclusion

Just as Oprah, if you are invariably striving to achieve greatness in all life aspects, you must maintain a couple of healthy habits. If Oprah's journey inspires you, then flexing to the above routine might be your thing. Who knows!

Chapter 3:
5 Ways To Adopt Right Attitude For Success

Being successful is a few elements that require hard work, dedication, and a positive attitude. It requires building your resilience and having a clear idea of your future ahead. Though it might be hard to decide your life forward, a reasonable manner is something that comes naturally to those who are willing to give their all. Adopting a new attitude doesn't always mean to change yourself in a way but, it has more meaning towards changing your mindset to an instinct. That is when you get stressed or overworked is because of an opposing point of view on life.

With success comes a great sense of dealing with things. You become more professional, and you feel the need to achieve more in every aspect. Don't be afraid to be power-hungry. But, it also doesn't mean to be unfair. Try to go for a little more than before, each step ahead. Make your hard work or talent count in every aspect. Make yourself a successful person in a positive manner, so you'll find yourself making the most of yourself. And don't give up on the things you need in life.

1. **Generate Pragmatic Impressions**

"The first impression is the last impression." It's true that once you've introduced yourself to the person in front of you, there is only a tiny chance that you'll get to introduce yourself again. So, choosing the correct wording while creating an impression is a must. You need to be optimistic about yourself and inform the other person about you in a way that influences them. An impression that leaves an effect on them, so they will willingly meet you again. A person must be kind and helpful towards its inferior and respectful towards their superior. This is one of the main characteristics for a person to be a successful man or woman. And with a negative attitude, the opposite occurs. People are more inclined to work without you. They nearly never consider you to work with them and try to contact you as little as possible. So, a good impression is significant.

2. Be True To Your Words

Choose your wording very carefully, because once said, it can't be taken back. Also, for a successful life, commitment is always an important rule. Be true to what you said to a person. Make them believe that they can trust you comfortably. So, it would be best if you chose your words. Don't commit if you can't perform. False commitment leads to loss of customers and leads to the loss of your impression as a successful worker. Always make sure that you fulfill your commands and promises to your clients and make them satisfied with your performance. It leads to a positive mindset and a dedication to work towards your goal.

3. A Positive Personal Life

Whatever you may be doing in your professional life can impact your personal life too. Creating the right mindset professionally also helps you to keep a positive attitude at home. It allows you to go forward with the proper consultation with your heart. It will make you happier. You'll desire to achieve more in life because you'll be satisfied with your success. It will push to go furthermore. It will drive you towards the passion for desiring more. Hard work and determination will continue to be your support, and you will be content will your heart. By keeping a good attitude, you'll be helping yourself more than helping others.

4. Be Aggressive and Determined

Becoming goal-oriented is one of the main factors evolving success in your life. If you are not determined to do your work, you'll just accept things the way others present you. It will leave you in misery and deeply dissatisfied with yourself. Similarly, you'll tend to do something more your way if you are goal-oriented and not how others want. You'll want to shale everything according to your need, and you become delighted with yourself and the result of your hard work. Always keep a clear view of your next step as it will form you in to your true self. Don't just go with the flow, but try to change it according to your wants and needs.

5. Create Your Master Plan

Indeed, we can't achieve great things with only hard work. We will always need to add a factor or to in our business. But by imagining or strategizing, some plans might be helpful. With hard work and some solid projects, we will get our desired outcome. If not, at least we get something close. And if you chose the wrong option, then the amount of hard work won't matter. You'll never get what you want no matter the hard work. So, always make sure to make plans strategically.

Conclusion

By keeping a positive attitude, you'll not only be helpful to others but to yourself too. Make sure you keep the proper manner—a manner required to be a successful person. Do lots of achievements and try to prove yourself as much as possible. Try keeping a good impact on people around you in everything you do. Have the spirit and courage to achieve great heights. And be sure to make moat of yourself. Consistency is the key.

Chapter 4:
6 Ways To Adopt A Better Lifestyle For Long-Term Success

A good lifestyle leads to a good life. The important choices we make throughout our lives impact our future in numerous ways. The need to make ourselves better in every aspect of life and the primary ability to perform such a routine can be a lifestyle. There is no proper way to live written in a book; however, through our shared knowledge and our comprehension, we can shape a lifestyle that can be beneficial and exciting at the same time. Though there is no doubt that falling into a specific routine can be difficult but, maintaining a proper state is more critical for a successful life.

For long-term success, a good lifestyle is a priority. Almost everything we do in our lives directly or indirectly involves our future self. So, a man needs to become habitual of such things that can profit him in every way possible. To visualize a better you, You need to configure just about everything around you. And to change all the habits that may make you feel lagging. The most common feature of a better lifestyle for long-term success is determination.

1. Change In Pattern Of Your Life

It is good to shape a pattern of living from the start and forming good habits, engaging yourself in profitable practice, and choosing a healthier custom. It feels impossible to change something you have already been habitual of, but willpower is the key. With some motivation and dedication, you can change yourself into a better version of yourself. You are choosing what might be suitable for you and staying determined on that thought. The first step is to let go of harmful things slowly because letting go of habits and patterns that you are used to can be challenging. After some, sometime you will notice yourself letting go of things more easily.

2. Take Your Time

Time is an essential factor when it comes to forming a lifestyle for a successful life. Time can seem to slow through the process, making us think that it may have been stopped in our most difficult moments. Similarly, making us feel it goes flying by when our life is relaxed and at ease. Time never stops for anyone. It is crucial to make sure we make most of our time and consume it in gaining more knowledge and power. Take time to inform your lifestyle, but not more than required. We are taking things at a moderate pace so you can both enjoy life and do work.

3. Don't Always Expect Things To Go Your Way

As much as we humans like to get our hopes high, we can't always expect things to go our way. Even things we have worked hard for can sometimes go downhill. It is at times overconfidence, but sometimes it can be pure bad luck. We can't get disheartened by something that was not meant to go a specific way. Don't expect perfection in all the work you do. Staying patient is the walk towards the reward. And making the best out of the worst can be the only way to get yourself going.

4. Don't Be Afraid To Ask For Help

It is human nature to ask each other for help now and then. If it comes to this point, don't be afraid to ask for help yourself. Ask someone superior to aid you on matters you find difficult. Don't hesitate to ask your inferiors who might have more knowledge than you in some certain customs. Help them, too, if needed. Ask them to assist you out on points, but never make them do the whole project. Don't make someone do something you wouldn't do yourself.

5. Be Prompt In Everything

Lagging behind your work can be the worst possible habit you could raise. Make yourself punctual in every aspect. Make sure you are on time everywhere. Either it's to wake up in the morning or to go to a meeting. Laziness can never be proven good for you or your dream towards a prosperous lifestyle. Respect time, and it shall respect you. Show your colleges that they can depend on you to show up on time and take responsibility for work. You would rather wait than making others wait for you. That will show you seriousness toward your business.

6. Keep A Positive Attitude

Keeping a positive attitude can lead to a positive lifestyle. Be happy with yourself in every context, and make sure that everything you do has your complete confidence. Be thankful to all who surround you. Keep a positive attitude, whether it be a home or office. Speak with your superiors with respect and make yourself approachable around inferiors. Your positive mindset can affect others in a way too. They will become more inclined towards you, and they can easily suggest you help someone.

Conclusion

Just about everything in your life affects your future in a way or other, so make sure that you do all you can to make yourself worth the praise. Keep your lifestyle simple but effective. Try to do as much as possible for yourself and make time to relax as well. For long-term success, willpower is the most important; make sure you have it. Keep your headlight and calm for the upcoming difficulties and prepare yourself to face almost everything life throws at you.

Chapter 5:

10 Habits of Lewis Hamilton

One thing is certain about Lewis Hamilton: he is a legend. He is a four-time Formula One World Champion who knows how to win on the track and in life. He is widely lauded as one of the best drivers of his generation, if not all time. In 2008, he became the youngest champion in history, winning the final turn of the season's final race.

He raced in Formula One for three decades, winning a record-equalling seven world championships, triple-figure pole positions, and a knighthood. You're surely aware that Lewis oozes driving talent, but there's much more to Hamilton than what he does behind the wheel. Here are the ten habits of Lewis Hamilton.

1. Executes Under Pressure

Racing drivers like Lewis must control and remain calm despite driving at speeds up to 230 miles per hour in a sports car that may reach temperatures of 50 degrees. With limited space and vision, you can imagine how hectic it is for him to composure himself to adapt, make split-second decisions, and win.

2. Keep Your Eyes on the Price

As a child, Lewis always wanted to be a race car driver. He even met his future boss, Ron Dennis, as a toddler and promised him that he'd be racing his cars in the future. With his attention and persistence, he was able to turn that goal into reality. How determined and focused are you in attaining your goals? Keep your eventual aim in sight at all times!

3. Technology Is Everything

Formula one racing is a technology-driven sport in which a minor flaw in the car can alter the race's outcome. Hamilton and his team are always ahead of others with well-researched data for optimizing his performance. To place your content in the driver's seat for success, it must be easily available, properly categorized, and in the proper format, which is why the platform you deal with must be intelligent, smart, and dependable.

4. Discipline Pays Off

Lewis Hamilton is one of the world's most disciplined athletes. While some people may not consider Formula one racing to be a sport in which you must be in peak physical condition to be successful, Lewis treats his physical fitness as a shrine for his mental health lucidity as mental health is key to racing. His commitment to healthy food and consistent training has helped him win 43 Formula One races throughout his career.

5. Put in the Effort

Lewis is all about dedication to excellence. "You start training in December, start testing at the end of January and through the entire month of February, and then you go to the season," he explained. You're always on the move. How committed are you to attain your most important goals? Small steps lead to big steps, and big steps lead to bigger steps.

6. Dispatch, Adapt and Enhance

When Lewis achieves something, he celebrates his victory debriefing, analyses his performance, and learns how they may have improved their racing plan. Lewis Hamilton is the best because of his relentless, determined pursuit of perfection. It would be best to always debrief with a reliable team, react to problems and develop your techniques, and stay ahead of the competition.

7. Physical and Mental Health First

Lewis is always trying to stay optimistic and healthy for his body, mind, soul, and spirit. It's hard to step back from doing something you love most but look at the bigger picture. Instead of grumbling or worrying about the future, step back and examine yourself-accessing and confronting your current issues.

8. Keep the Right People

While it appears that you get to tour the world and explore in Formula One, you spend more time alone. Lewis spends most of his time with Angela-his best friend, trainer, and physiotherapist. She exudes positive energy and always keeps him strong and motivated, so he can focus on remaining competitive.

9. Don't Gauge Yourself Against Others.

Lewis doesn't consider other drivers in terms of inspiration, motivation, or anything else. He's always sailing his boat towards becoming the best he can be. Devote your energy and time in improving yourself for yourself, not for others.

10. Self-Belief Is Key

Rosanna once asked Lewis, "Is there ever a time when you doubt your own abilities?" "No," Lewis said. Without delving too deeply into this, it's a given that you should believe in yourself in the same way Hamilton does.

Conclusion

Lewis Hamilton relentless determination towards being the best is what keeps him a champion. And just like him, always work towards perfecting what you are good at.

Chapter 6:

8 Steps To Develop Beliefs That Will Drive you To Success

'Success' is a broad term. There is no universal definition of success, it varies from person to person considering their overall circumstances. We can all more or less agree that confidence plays a key role in it, and confidence comes from belief.

Even our most minute decisions and choices in life are a result of believing in some specific outcome that we have not observed yet.

However, merely believing in an ultimate success will not bring fortune knocking at your door. But, it certainly can get you started—take tiny steps that might lead you towards your goal. Now, since we agree that having faith can move you towards success, let's look at some ways to rewire your brain into adopting productive beliefs.

Here are 8 Steps to Develop Beliefs That Will Drive You To Success:

1. **Come Up With A Goal**

Before you start, you need to decide what you want to achieve first. Keep in mind that you don't have to come up with something very specific right away because your expectations and decisions might change over time. Just outline a crude sense of what 'Achievement' and 'Success' mean to you in the present moment.

Begin here. Begin now. Work towards getting there.

2. **Put Your Imagination Into Top Gear**

"Logic will take you from A to B. Imagination will take you everywhere", said Albert Einstein.

Imagination is really important in any scenario whatsoever. It is what makes us humans different from animals. It is what gives us a reason to move forward—it gives us hope. And from that hope, we develop the will to do things we have never done before.

After going through the first step of determining your goal, you must now imagine yourself being successful in the near future. You have to literally picture yourself in the future, enjoying your essence of fulfilment as vividly as you can. This way, your ultimate success will appear a lot closer and realistic.

3. **Write Notes To Yourself**

Writing down your thoughts on paper is an effective way to get those thoughts stuck in your head for a long time. This is why children are encouraged to write down what is written in the books instead of memorizing them just by reading. You have to write short, simple, motivating notes to yourself that will encourage you to take actions towards your success. It doesn't matter whether you write in a notebook, or on your phone or wherever—just write it. On top of that, occasionally read what you've written and thus, you will remain charged with motivation at all times.

4. **Make Reading A Habit**

There are countless books written by successful people just so that they can share the struggle and experience behind their greatest achievements. In such an abundance of manuscripts, you may easily find books that portray narratives similar to your life and circumstances. Get reading and expand your knowledge. You'll get never-thought-before ideas that will guide you through your path to success. Reading such books will tremendously strengthen your faith in yourself, and in your success. Read what other successful people believed in—what drove them. You might even find newer beliefs to hold on to. No wonder why books are called 'Man's best friend'.

5. **Talk To People Who Motivates You**

Before taking this step, you have to be very careful about who you talk to. Basically, you have to speak out your goals and ambitions in life to someone who will be extremely supportive of you. Just talk to them about what you want, share your beliefs and they will motivate you from time to time towards success. They will act as powerful reminders. Being social beings, no human can ever reject the gist of motivation coming from another human being—especially when that is someone whom you can rely on comfortably. Humans have been the sole supporter of each other since eternity.

6. **Make A Mantra**

Self-affirming one-liners like 'I can do it', 'Nothing can stop me', 'Success is mine' etc. will establish a sense of firm confidence in your subconscious mind. Experts have been speculative about the power of our subconscious mind for long. The extent of what it can do is still beyond our grasp. But nonetheless, reciting subtle mantras isn't a difficult task. Do it a couple of times every day and it will remain in your mind for ages, without you giving any conscious thought to it. Such subconscious affirmations may light you up in the right moment and show you the path to success when you least expect it.

7. **Reward Yourself From Time To Time**

Sometimes, your goals might be too far-fetched and as a result, you'll find it harder to believe in something so improbable right now. In a situation like this, what you can do is make short term objectives that ultimately lead to your main goal and for each of those objectives achieved, treat yourself with a reward of any sort—absolutely anything that pleases you. This way, your far cry success will become more apparent to you in the present time. Instant rewards like these will also keep you motivated and make you long for more. This will drive you to believe that you are getting there, you are getting closer and closer to success.

8. Having Faith In Yourself

Your faith is in your hands alone. How strongly you believe in what you deserve will motivate you. It will steer the way for self-confidence to fulfill your inner self. You may be extremely good at something but due to the lack of faith in your own capabilities, you never attempted it—how will you ever know that you were good at that? Your faith in yourself and your destined success will materialize before you through these rewards that you reserve for yourself. You absolutely deserve this!

Final Thoughts

That self-confidence and belief and yourself, in your capabilities and strengths will make you work towards your goal. Keep in mind that whatever you believe in is what you live for. At the end of the day, each of us believed in something that made us thrive, made us work and move forward. Some believed in the military, some believed in maths, some believed in thievery—everyone had a belief which gave them a purpose—the purpose of materializing their belief in this world. How strongly you hold onto your belief will decide how successful you will become.

Chapter 7:
6 Ways On How To Change Your Body Language To Attract Success

"If you want to find the truth, do not listen to the words coming to you. Rather see the body language of the speaker. It speaks the facts not audible." - Bhavesh Chhatbar.

Our body language is exceptionally essential as 60-90% of our communication with others is nonverbal. If properly used, it can be our key to more tremendous success. We focus more on our business plans, our marketing drives, and our spreadsheets rather than considering our facial expressions, posture, or what our physical gestures might be saying about us. Our mindset also plays a role in how our body language expresses itself. No matter how impressive our words maybe, if we are sending a negative signal with our body language, we would eventually lose the opportunities of gaining more success.

Here is a list to help you change your body language to attract more success.

1. **The Power of Voice**

Your personal voice has a huge impact and can literally make or break your success. It is one of the most direct routes to empower your communication. The pitch of your voice, its timbre, cadence, volume, and the speed with which you speak, are all influential factors that will ensure how convincing you are and how people will judge your character. Lowering your voice at the right moment or injecting some spontaneity into it when needed will enhance your credibility and lend you an air of intelligence. We must fill our voices with our range and depth if we want others and ourselves to take us seriously.

2. The Power of Listening

An excellent speaking skill represents only half of the leadership expression. The other half is mastering your art in listening. While a good listener is incredibly rare, it is essential to keep our ears open to any valuable information that is often silently transmitted. When we start listening attentively to others, we begin to notice what a person is saying and decode accurately what they don't say. You will also begin to realize what the other person is thinking or whether their attitude is positive or hostile towards you. With these particular observations, you will likely attune to another person and create the bond crucial to a successful working life.

3. The Necessity for Emotional Intelligence

The skill of acute listening develops our emotional intelligence, the intuition to ascertain the objective reality of the situation. When we lack emotional intelligence, we might misinterpret situations and fail to decipher what might be needed. Emotional intelligence deepens our empathy. It gives us the ability to be present and listen to someone when they need it the most. It is the single best predictor of performance in the workplace and can be the most vital driver of personal excellence and leadership. Our understanding of emotional intelligence will vastly improve our internal relations and can also deepen our sense of personal fulfillment and professional accomplishment.

4. The Power of Eye Contact

Making eye contact and holding it is seen as a sign of confidence, and the other person is felt valued. It increases your chance of being trustful and respected as they tend to listen to you more attentively and feel comfortable giving you their insights. You may be shy, an introvert, or might have heard that it's impolite to maintain eye contact with a superior. But in many parts of the world, business people expect you to maintain eye contact 50-60% of the time. Here's a simple tip: when you meet someone, look into their eyes long enough to notice their eye color.

5. Talk With Your Hands

There's a region in our brain called the Broca's area, which is essential and active during our speech production and when we wave our hands. Gestures are integrally linked to speech, so gesturing while talking can speed up your thinking. Using hand gestures while talking can improve verbal content as well as make your speechless hesitant. You will see that it will help you form clearer thoughts with more declarative language and speak in tighter sentences.

6. Strike A Power Pose

Research conducted at Harvard and Columbia Business Schools into the effects of body posture and confidence show that holding your body in expansive high-power poses (such as leaning back with hands behind the head or standing with legs and arms stretched wide open) for only as little as two minutes can stimulate high levels of testosterone (a hormone linked to power) and lower levels of cortisol (a stress hormone). You will look and feel more confident and inevitable, leading to an increased feeling of energy and a high tolerance for risk.

Conclusion

Most of our body language and movement are subconscious, so it can be challenging to retrain ourselves away from habits we have had for years. Still, we must try to master our body language, too, with the art of public speaking. Regular practice Is the key to success and the quickest route to attain confident body language as with any other skill. Practice them in your day-to-day life so that they may become deep-rooted. Be less compliant and step into an edgier, emboldened, and more genuine you.

Chapter 8:
9 Habits of Highly Successful People

Success comes to people who deserve it. I bet you have heard this statement quite a few times, right? So, what does it mean exactly? Does it mean that you are either born worthy or unworthy of success? Absolutely not. Everyone is born worthy, but the one thing that makes some people successful is their winning habits and their commitment to these habits.

Today, we will learn how to master ten simple habits and behaviors that will help you become successful.

1. Be an Avid Learner

If you didn't know, almost all of the most successful people in the world are avid learners. So, do not shy away from opportunities when it comes to learning. Wake up each day and look forward to learning new things, and in no time, I bet you will experience how enriching it really is. Also, learning new things has the effect of revitalizing a person. So, if you want to have more knowledge to kickstart your journey in the right direction, here are some things that you can do - make sure to read, even if it is just a page or two, daily. It could be anything that interests you. I personally love reading self-help books. If you are not that much of a reader, you can even listen to a podcast, watch an informative video, or sign up for a course. Choose what piques your interest, and just dive into it!

2. Failure is the Pillar of Success

Most people are afraid to delve into something new, start a new chapter of their lives, and chase after their dreams – all because they are scared to fail. If you are one of those people who are scared to fail, well, don't be! Because what failure actually does is prepares you to achieve your dream. It just makes sure that you are able to handle the success when you finally have it. So when you accept that failure is an inevitable part of your journey, you will be able to plan the right course of action to tackle it instead of just being too scared to move forward. Successful people are never scared of failure; They just turn it around by seeing it as an opportunity to learn.

3. Get Up Early

I bet you have heard this a couple of thousand times already! But whoever told you so was not lying. Almost all successful individuals are early risers! They say that starting the morning right ensures a fruitful day ahead. It is true! Think about it, on the day you get up early, you feel a boost of productivity as compared to when you wake up late and have to struggle against the clock. You will have plenty of time and a good mood to go through the rest of the day which will give you better outcomes. All you have to do is set up a bedtime reminder. This is going to make sure that you enough rest to get up in the morning instead of snoozing your alarm on repeat! Not a morning person? Don't worry. I have got you covered! Start slow and set the alarm 15 minutes before when you usually wake up. It doesn't sound like much, eh? But trust me, you will be motivated to wake up earlier when you see how much difference 15 minutes can make to your day.

4. Have Your Own Morning Ritual

Morning rituals are the most common habit among achievers. It will pump you up to go through the day with a bang! You just have to make a routine for yourself and make sure to follow it every day. You can take inspiration from the morning routines of people you look up to but remember it has to benefit you. So you might be wondering, *What do I include in the ritual?* I would suggest you make your bed first thing in the morning. This might not sound as great a deal, but hey, it is a tested and approved method to boost your productivity. It is even implemented in the military. Doing this will motivate you as you get a sense of achievement as you have completed a task as soon as you woke up. After that, it could be anything that will encourage you, such as a walk, a workout session, reading, journaling, or meditating.

5. Stop Procrastinating

From delaying one task to not keeping up with your deadlines, procrastination becomes a deadly habit. It becomes almost unstoppable! Did you know, most people fail to achieve their dreams even if they have the potential just because of procrastination? Well, they do. And you might not want to become one of them. They say, "Old habits die hard," true, but they do die if you want them to. Procrastination has to be the hardest thing we have to deal with, even though we hey created it in the first place. Trust me, I speak from experience!

So what do you do to stop this? Break your task into small bite-sized pieces. Sometimes, it is just the heaviness of the task that keeps us from doing it. Take breaks in between to keep yourself motivated.

Another thing that you can do is the "minute rule." Divide your tasks by how much time they take. The tasks that take less than 5 minutes, you do it right then. Then you can bigger tasks into small time frames and complete them. Make sure you do not get too lost in the breaks, though!

6. Set Goals

I cannot even begin to tell you how effective goal setting is. A goal gives you the right direction and motivation. It also gives you a sense of urgency to do a task that is going to just take your productivity level from 0 to 10 in no time!

So how do you set goals? Simple. Think about the goals you want to achieve and write them down. But make sure that you set realistic goals. If you find it difficult, don't worry. Start small and slow. Start by making a to-do list for the day. You will find out soo that the satisfaction in ticking those off your list is unbelievable. It will also drive you to tick more of them off!

7. Make Your Health a Priority

Health is Wealth. Yes, it is a fact! When you give your body the right things and make it a priority, it gives you back by keeping you and your mind healthy. I bet you've heard the saying "You are what you eat," and by "eat," it does not simply mean to chew and swallow! It also means that you need to feed your body, soul, and mind with things you want them to be like. Read, listen, learn, and eat healthy. You could set a goal to eat clean for the week. Or workout at least for 10 minutes. And see for yourself how it gives you the energy to smash those goals you've been holding off! Also, great news – you can have cheat days once a week!

8. Plan Your Day the Night Before

"When you fail to plan, you plan to fail." People who succeed in life are not by mere coincidence or luck. It is the result of detailed, focused planning. So, you need to start planning your way to success too. Before you sleep tonight, ask yourself, *What is the most important thing that I have to do tomorrow?* Plan what assignments, meetings, or classes you have to complete. Planning ahead will not only make you organized and ready, it also highly increases your chances to succeed. So, don't forget to plan your day tonight!

9. Master the Habit Loop

Behavioral expert, BJ Fogg, explains that habits are formed around three elements: Cue, Routine, and Reward. Cue is the initial desire that motivates your behavior. Routine is the action you take. And the reward is the pleasure you gain after completion. So why am I telling you all of this? Because this habit loop is how we are wired. It is what motivates us. We seek pleasure and avoid pain. And you can use this loop to your advantage! Let's say you want to finish an assignment. Think of the reason why you want to. Maybe you don't want to fall behind someone or want to impress someone. It could be anything! Now time for you to set your rewards. It could be eating a slice of cheesecake or watching an episode of your favorite series after you've finished. Rewards motivate you when you slack off. Play around until you find a combination that works best for you. You will also need a cue; it could be anything like a notification on your phone, an email, or simply your desire. You can set a cue yourself by creating a reminder.

Habits are what make a man. I hope you follow these habits and start your journey the right way to becoming successful in life.

PART 3

Chapter 1:
6 Tricks to become more aware of your strengths.

"Strength and growth come only through continuous effort and struggle." - Napoleon Hill.

While it is true that we tend to focus more on our weaknesses than on our strengths, it is also true that we should polish our strengths more than our weaknesses. This in no way means that we should consider ourselves superior to others and start looking away from that we have flaws. Unfortunately, most of us don't spend much time on self-reflection and self-awareness. But they are the vital aspects if we are thinking of improving ourselves in any way.

Here are 6 Tricks to become more aware of your strengths:

1. Decide to be more self-aware

Human beings are complicated creatures. Our minds are designed so that we tend to absorb more negative than positive thoughts about ourselves and others. For this reason, self-awareness is perhaps the most crucial thing in an individual's life. Self-awareness is the ability to look deep inside of yourself and monitor your emotions and reactions. It is the ability to allow yourself to be aware of your strengths, weaknesses, as well as your triggers, motivators, and other characteristics. We'll help you find a set of tricks and techniques that you can apply to polish your strengths in a self-awareness way; and how to use your strengths in a promising way.

2. Meditation:

The first thought that will come to your mind would be, "Is this person crazy? How can meditation help us improve our strengths?" But hear me out. The fresh breeze of the morning when everything is at peace, and you sit there inhaling all the good energy in and the bad energy out, your mind and thoughts would automatically become slow-paced and calm. Once you get to relax with yourself, you can analyze the things that have been happening in your life and develop possible solutions on how you can deal with them using your strengths. The positive energy and calming mood you will get after meditating would help you make your decisions wisely when you are under pressure and your mind is in chaos.

3. Labeling your thoughts:

More often, our thoughts reflect on our behavior and what makes us fail or succeed in life. People can genuinely relate to a situation where they could have possibly thought about a worst-case scenario, but in the end, nothing as such happened. Our anxiety and hopelessness don't come from the situation we are struggling with, but rather our thoughts make us believe in the worst possible things that could happen to us. But we're stronger than we give ourselves credit for. We have the power to control our negative thoughts and turn them into positive ones. We can list all the ideas and thinking that provide us with stress and tension and then label them as either useful or useless. If the particular thought is causing a significant effect in your life, you can work towards it to make your life better and less anxious. Know your priorities and take help from your strengths to tackle the problems.

4. Befriending your fears:

There's not a single person on this planet who isn't afraid of something. Be it the fear of losing your loved ones or any phobias of either animal, insects, heights, closed spaces, etc. There are also so many fears related to our self-worth and whether we are good enough, skilled enough, or deserving enough of anything. To accept these fears and work towards overcoming them is perhaps the most powerful thing one could do. It takes so much of a person's strength and willpower to befriend fear, reduce it, and finally eliminate it. Most of the time, we end up in situations that we always feared, and then we have to take quick actions and make wise decisions. To remain calm in such cases and use your strengths and experiences to tackle whatever's in front of you is a remarkable quality found in only a few. But we can also achieve and polish this quality by strengthening our minds and preparing ourselves to get us out of situations wisely and effectively. To be patient and look into the problems from every angle is the critical component of this one.

5. **Watching your own movie:**

Narrating your life experiences to yourself or a close friend and telling yourself and them how far you have come can boost your self-confidence immensely. You should go in flashbacks and try to remember all the details of your life. You will find that there were some moments you felt immense joy and some moments where you felt like giving up. But with all the strength that you were collecting along the way, you endured the possible tortures and struggles and challenges and eventually rose again. So you should focus and be well aware of how you tackle those situations, what powers you have, and the strengths that couldn't let you give up but face everything. Once you have found the answers to the above questions, like for example, it was your patience and bravery that helped you through it, or it was your wise and speedy decisions that made it all effective, you can understand what strengths you have and make use of them later in life too.

6. **Motivate yourself:**

We should stop looking for others to notice how great we did or stop waiting for a round of applause or a pat on the back from them. Instead, we should motivate ourselves every time we fall apart, and we should have the energy to pick ourselves back up again. The feeling of satisfaction we get after completing a task or helping someone, that feeling is what we should strive for. We should become proud of ourselves and our strengths, as well as our weaknesses, that they helped us transform into the person we are today. We should never feel either superior or inferior to others. Everyone has their own pace and their own struggles. Our strengths should not only be for ourselves but for others too. Kindness, empathy, hospitality, being there for people, patience, courage, respect are all the qualities that one must turn into their strengths.

Conclusion:

The key to perfection is self-awareness. There's a fine line between who you are and who you strive to become; it can be achieved by becoming aware of your strengths, polishing them, and creating a sense of professional as well as personal development. Your strengths motivate you to try new things, achieve new skills, become a better version of yourself. Your strengths are what keeps you positive, motivated, help you to maintain your stress better, aid you in your intuitive decision making, and command you to help others as well. It inspires you to become a better person.

Chapter 2:
10 Habits of Elon Musk

An alternator, Inventor, and a Disruptor! These phrases and Elon Musk are very synonymous. As a founder of such platforms as PayPal, Tesla, and SpaceX, Musk is worth being associated with these words! Every time Musk sits in his office means surprising the world with a new Corvette, as he did recently, by launching the 50th SpaceX. Whether you want to be an inventive business person or an employee, you can learn a lot from this authentic Iron Man.

These ten habits will uncover how Musk achieved his dreams, and so can you.

1. Before life gets in your way, take risks.

The perfect time to be an entrepreneur is when you are young. Responsibilities grow as you get older. Musk always encourages young people to take risks by doing something daring. Because as one gets old, responsibilities pile up.

Risk-taking has an impact on your family and children as you become older. Not to mention that you'll have less free time. Instead, take chances now when you don't have any other obligations or time constraints

2. To Lead, Read

Formal education may come to an end, but your street smartness shouldn't. As Musk said, "You have no idea things you don't know that are out there." This is entirely true. Musk read the entire *Britannica Encyclopedia* as a child while most of us were reading the *Goodnight Moon*. His reading habit has only accelerated as he has gotten older. Are you able to claim the same position about your reading patterns?

Immerse yourself in the literature that will broaden your scope and provide you with new ideas and perspectives. It should come as no surprise that the best learners are also the best earners in society.

3. Ignite the Midnight Energy.

As dedicated as he is to his work, Musk's work ethic is notoriously perfect. He works for up to a hundred hours across his many businesses. You don't have to do the same, but keep Elon in mind the next time you're fatigued or when you aren't motivated. He is an example of what pushing yourself looks like. If you do not follow suit, you may be squandering your potential.

4. Make a Plan for Success, but Be Prepared To Fail.

There is no such thing as a successful crystal ball. Even Musk had no idea how his Tesla Motors would fare. However, as he put it, "When something is valuable enough, you can try even though failure is the likely outcome." It would help if you made every effort to have your dreams come true. But also be prepared for anything just in case things don't work out as planned. With a backup plan in place, it is easier to overcome the failures.

5. Complaining Is a Game-Changer.

The majority of individuals grumble about traffic. Elon Musk is not one of them. Rather than complaining about the situation, Musk sought a remedy. This gave rise to an actual Company, which aims to reduce traffic congestion by building a subway system. Creating a future for yourself is the most effective strategy to attain the outcomes you desire. This was a lesson that enabled Kogan of Wolfie to grow his business. "Complaints are an indication that there is a problem that needs to be solved," he explains. "Listening to grievances is a fantastic method to come up with fresh ideas that people genuinely need."

6. Be Yourself.

"Don't just go with the flow," Musk advised. Most of the notable thriving businesses concentrate on developing breakthroughs. They do not attempt to outrun the opponent. Affirming this notion is the CEO and founder of the Viral Content Marketing-Jonny Videl. "Going viral isn't something that happens by chance," he explains. "Instead of pursuing others, stand firmly by putting your focus on whatever makes you unique.

7. Competing With Anyone Else Makes You Bitter.

In life, there is always a second chance for improvement. As Musk noted, it's critical to have a feedback mechanism in place, where you're constantly contemplating what you have achieved and how to do it better. That, I believe, is the most crucial nugget of advice: embrace continuous questioning of every detail of what you have done and consider ways of doing things better. Don't be afraid of unfavorable feedback because it frequently uncovers new ideas.

8. Treat Your Stakeholders As if They Were Family.

Treat your co-workers or your customers as they were your own. Musk, for example, is always thanking and appreciating his customers on Twitter daily. People will always notice modest gestures, no matter how small they are. Most successful people like Maulik Parekh-President and CEO of SPi CRM, have emulated this habit, and it seems to be working. Speaking to an interview, Maulik noted, "Our personnel is our most valuable asset. If we look after them, they will look after the business. What we do for our employees is what we do for your clients." Take time outside your corner office to develop the foundations of your firm through employee and customer interactions.

9. Spending All of Your Money on Advertising

Is Not a Good Idea.

Musk does not squander money on advertising. Instead, he asks, "Will this activity result in a better product or service?" This one pain to hear as a marketer. But try to understand Musk's reasoning. A high-quality product will generate a lot of positive word of mouth. Concentrate on that first, and the rest will fall into place.

10. See the Best in Everything That You Do.

To do good, you don't have to transform the world entirely. However, you should constantly strive to deliver genuine value. According to Musk, producing something of great importance, however little it is, if it achieves the modest bit of good for a huge crowd, then it's acceptable. Things don't have to transform the world to be perfect. See the positivity in every detail of your work. No matter how small it is, it will motivate you.

Conclusion

Whatever your life goals are, emulating Elon Musk's habits and way of thinking can help you get there. The extra work you put into reaching your life goals will have a significant impact on your future.

Chapter 3:
7 Reasons Your beliefs are holding you back

You know that you have immense potential in your heart, and you are also working hard to attain your desired results, but something still doesn't fit right. Your beliefs might be consciously or unconsciously sabotaging your potential through your actions. This might create the less-than-desirable results that are holding you back from your real success.

Here are some 5 beliefs that might be getting in your way. Observe and analyze them, and start getting rid of them so that your path to success becomes easy and thorn-free.

1. **Beliefs Are More Powerful Than You Think**

"Beliefs have the power to create and the power to destroy. Human beings have the awesome ability to take any experience of their lives and create a meaning that disempowers them or one that can literally save their lives." - Tony Robbins. To change our lives, we first have to change our mindset and what we believe in so dearly. Challenging your beliefs is the key element to improve yourself. If we look around us, we might find a few limiting beliefs in the blink of an eye.

2. **Everyone will get ahead of me if I rest.**

This is perhaps the most crucial limiting belief that the majority of people go through. Many of us think that if we take some time off for ourselves, we'll fall behind in life, and everyone will get ahead of us, crushing us beneath them. For this particular reason, we stop focusing on our needs and necessities and burns out all of our energy on things that should come as second on our lists. Instead, we should convert our "shoulds" into "musts" and focus on ourselves too. Meditating for an hour, going to the gym, taking some time off for hanging out with friends or watching a movie alone, reading a book that's not connected to your work, these all are necessary to sustain life. Making excuses for not taking any time off for yourself and working day and night tirelessly will drain your energy or become a problem for your health; likewise, you will be tired physically and mentally and wouldn't be able to do your tasks on time.

3. Everyone is succeeding in life but me.

With the increasing social media norms and the lives of celebrities on every cover page, or seeing everyone around you figuring their lives out and enjoying themselves, you might feel that you are the only one who hasn't got a thing right. Unfortunately, human nature shows the world our successes and happiness rather than telling them our weak, struggling phases and vulnerability. Comparing yourself to those around you or any celebrity or influencer from social media may become a downward spiral for you when you are feeling confused and lost. Believing that everyone has it easy and you are the only one struggling could make you feel demotivated and depressed. This would, in turn, make you lazy, and you would eventually stop working towards your goal and passion.

4. I can never be good enough.

This limiting belief is the most common one among the people. Initially, they would give their all to a new job, a new relationship, or a new task. Then, if things wouldn't work out for them, they would just blame their performance and themselves and would label it as "I'm not good enough for this." This often leads to being anxious and finding perfection in things. And if failed to achieve this, one starts to procrastinate, thinking that their energies and efforts will eventually go to waste anyway. The little voice inside your head telling you that you're not good enough might also make you believe that you're not skilled enough or talented enough for the job or not deserving enough to be with the person you like. As a result, you pull yourself back and miss out on any opportunities offered to you.

5. I am capable enough to do everything myself.

We're often fooled by the idea that we don't need anyone's help, and we can figure out everything independently. This approach is majorly toxic as we all need a helping hand now and then. No one walks on the path of success alone. You may feel ashamed or guilty in asking for help or may think that you will be rejected or let down, or may think of yourself as the superior creature who knows everything and are not ready to listen to anyone else. All this might bring you down at one point in your life. We should always be open to any criticism and feedback and should never shy away from asking any help or advice from the people we trust and from the people we get inspired from.

6. The tiny voice becomes too loud sometimes

Limiting beliefs does impede us in some way. There's always this tiny voice in the back of our heads that keeps whispering thoughts and ideas into our minds. Most of what the voice tells us are negative stuff, and the worst part is that we actually start to believe in all of that. "You can never lose weight; stop trying. You're unattractive, and you won't find your significant other any time soon. You don't have the mindset or money to start up your own business; get yourself a 9-5 job instead." All of these, and much more, are what pulls us back from the things that we want to say or the stuff that we want to do.

7. The time isn't right.

The time isn't right, and believe me, it never will be. You're wasting your life away thinking that you will get married, lose your weight, learn a new skill, start your own business, all when the time will be correct. But there's no such as the right time. You either start doing what you want or sit on the side-lines and watch someone else do it. The right time is here and now. It would be best if you started doing the things you want until you make up your mind that you want to do it. You don't have to wait for a considerable amount of money to start a business; start with a small one instead. You don't have to settle down first to get married; find someone who will grow with you and help you. You don't need to spend hours and hours in the gym to lose weight; start eating healthy. There is no right time for anything, but the time becomes right when you decide to change yourself and your life for the better.

Conclusion:

You can make a thousand excuses or find a million experiences to back up your beliefs, but truth be told, you should always be aware of the assumptions you are creating and how they may be affecting your life. For example, will your beliefs stop you from taking action towards your life? Or will you change them into new and creative opportunities to get the results you want?

Chapter 4:

7 Habits To Start Right Now

"We're what we do over and over again. Therefore, excellence is not an act, it is a habit." steven covey once said. Sometimes it can be disheartening to focus on the end goals and objectives if you don't really know if you play the wrong sport. Again, what are the rules? How do I gain and win success in this game? It's even harder when the goalpost moves, often when you think about advancement or changes in career or life.

Has anybody taken your idea back or not lauded you? Feeling uninspired and bored? Are you unhappy where you are? Still Uncertain? Looking to new trials? There several unique strategies that can incredibly ace up your desires and help you you're your personal as well as professional life. practices incredibly recommendable that can help you ace up and brighten your daily existence.

Here Are 7 Habits That You Need To Start Right Now.

1. Be proactive

This is power of choice. It's more than initiative to be proactive. Being or taking responsibility for your behaviour. Be it those in the past, present and the future. You must make decisions based on values and principles rather than on moods or circumstances. Proactive people are agents of change and they do not choose to be victims, reactive or guilty. They are doing this with the development and application of quatre unique human gifts—self-consciousness, consciousness, imagination, and a free will—and an Inside-Out approach to changing. They are determined to be the creative force that is the most fundamental decision ever made in their life.

2. Begin with the end in your mind

(Two measurements, one cut) Everything is created twice, first physically and mentally. Individuals, families, teams and organisations, create a mental view and a purpose for each project, shaping their own future. Without a clear purpose in mind, they do not live daily. The principles, values, relationships and purposes most important to them are mentally identified and committed. The highest form of mental creation for an individual, a family or an organization is a mission statement. The primary decision is because all other decisions are governed by it. There creates a culture of leadership in your goals or mission or vision and stick to the process.

3. First (organize + execute priorities) put First Things First.

The second or physical creation is putting first things first. The question is how the mindset is prepared and put in place (your purpose, vision, values, and most important priorities). First things don't come second nor will first things be coming in third. The most important thing is to keep and priotize the main thing.

4. Endeavour to understand than to be understood first

If you develop a listening first habit, you begin a true communication and relationship building instead of listening in an attempt to understand others. If others first feel understood, they feel valued and affirmed, defence, and opportunities to speak openly and be understood are reduced. To seek understanding requires kindness; to be understood requires courage. The balance between the two is effective.

5. A "we" thinking. Think of a win-win not a "me" win.

Thinking mutual benefit is a mood and heart that looks for shared advantage and depends on common regard in all cooperations. It's tied in with speculation regarding plenitude—an always growing "pie," a cornucopia of chance, abundance, and assets—instead of shortage and antagonistic rivalry. it's not reasoning egotistically (win-lose) or like a saint (lose-win). in your work and day to day life, individuals think reliantly—as far as "we," not "me." Thinking shared benefit supports compromise and assists people with looking for commonly useful arrangements. It's sharing data, force, acknowledgment, and prizes.

6. Synergism

Synergy is tied in with delivering a third other option—not my way, not your way, but rather a third way that is better compared to both of us would think of exclusively. it's the product of common regard—of understanding and in any event, commending each other's disparities in taking care of issues, taking advantage of chances. Synergistic groups and families flourish with singular qualities so the entire gets more prominent than the amount of the parts. Synergy is known for its creative cooperation.

7. Do something daily to renew and recharge

Honing the saw is about continually recharging yourself genuinely, intellectually, inwardly/socially, and profoundly. These are your four center human necessities; and honing your saw is tied in with accomplishing something consistently to keep up or upgrade yourself across every one of the four measurements. This is the Habit that expands our ability to live any remaining propensities for viability.

If you are willing able to follow up these habits, then be sure to get the desired goals more than ever. As surviving, and better though, winning via the regular seasons depends on this persistence.

Chapter 5:
6 Steps To Get Out of Your Comfort Zone

The year 2020 and 2021 have made a drastic change in all our lives, which might have its effect forever. The conditions of last year and a half have made a certain lifestyle choice for everyone, without having a say in it for us.

This new lifestyle has been a bit overwhelming for some and some started feeling lucky. Most of us feel comfortable working from home, and taking online classes while others want to have some access to public places like parks and restaurants.

But the pandemic has affected everyone more than once. And now we are all getting used to this relatively new experience of doing everything from home. Getting up every day to the same routine and the same environment sometimes takes us way back on our physical and mental development and creativity.

So one must learn to leave the comfort zone and keep themselves proactive. Here are some ways anyone can become more productive and efficient.

Everyone is always getting ready to change but never changing.

1. Remember your Teenage Self

People often feel nostalgic remembering those days of carelessness when they were kids and so oblivious in that teenage. But, little do they take for inspiration or motivation from those times. When you feel down, or when you don't feel like having the energy for something, just consider your teenage self at that time.

If only you were a teenager now, you won't be feeling lethargic or less motivated. Rather you'd be pushing harder and harder every second to get the job done as quickly as possible. If you could do it back then, you still can! All you need is some perspective and a medium to compare to.

2. Delegate or Mentor someone

Have you ever needed to have someone who could provide you some guidance or help with a problem that you have had for some time?

I'm sure, you weren't always a self-made man or a woman. Somewhere along the way, there was someone who gave you the golden quote that changed you consciously or subconsciously.

Now is the time for you to do the same for someone else. You could be a teacher, a speaker, or even a mentor who doesn't have any favors to ask in return. Once you get the real taste of soothing someone else's pain, you won't hesitate the next time.

This feeling of righteousness creates a chain reaction that always pushes you to get up and do good for anyone who could need you.

3. Volunteer in groups

The work of volunteering may seem pointless or philanthropic. But the purpose for you to do it should be the respect that you might get, but the stride to get up on your feet and help others to be better off.

Volunteering for flood victims, earthquake affectees or the starving people of deserts and alpines can help you understand the better purpose of your existence. This keeps the engine of life running.

4. Try New Things for a Change

Remember the time in Pre-school when your teachers got you to try drawing, singing, acting, sculpting, sketching, and costume parties. Those weren't some childish approach to keep you engaged, but a planned system to get your real talents and skills to come out.

We are never too old to learn something new. Our passions are unlimited just as our dreams are. We only need a push to keep discovering the new horizons of our creative selves.

New things lead to new people who lead to new places which might lead to new possibilities. This is the circle of life and life is ironic enough to rarely repeat the same thing again.

You never know which stone might lead you to a gold mine. So never stop discovering and experiencing because this is what makes us the supreme being.

5. Push Your Physical Limits

This may sound cliched, but it always is the most important point of them all. You can never get out of your comfort zone, till you see the world through the hard glass.

The world is always softer on one side, but the image on the other side is far from reality. You can't expect to get paid equally to the person who works 12 hours a day in a large office of hundreds of employees. Only if you have the luxury of being the boss of the office.

You must push yourself to search for opportunities at every corner. Life has always more and better to offer at each stop, you just have to choose a stop.

6. Face Your Fears Once and For All

People seem to have a list of Dos and Dont's. The latter part is mostly because of a fear or a vacant thought that it might lead to failure for several reasons.

You need a "Do it all" behavior in life to have an optimistic approach to everything that comes in your way.

What is the biggest most horrible thing that can happen if you do any one of these things on your list? You need to have a clear vision of the possible worst outcome.

If you have a clear image of what you might lose, now must try to go for that thing and remove your fear once and for all. Unless you have something as important as your life to lose, you have nothing to fear from anything.

No one can force you to directly go skydiving if you are scared of heights. But you can start with baby steps, and then, maybe, later on in life you dare to take a leap of faith.

"Life is a rainbow, you might like one color and hate the other. But that doesn't make it ugly, only less tempting".

All you need is to be patient and content with what you have today, here, right now. But, you should never stop aiming for more. And you certainly shouldn't regret it if you can't have or don't have it now.

People try to find their week spots and frown upon those moments of hard luck. What they don't realize is, that the time they wasted crying for what is in the past, could have been well spent for a far better future they could cherish for generations to come.

Chapter 6:
5 Habits of Bill Gates

Bill gates is a name synonymous with success. Who does not know Bill Gates? His footprints are everywhere. Students in elementary school look up to him as their role model. Those in high school and higher levels of education idolize him. He is a semi-god, everyone wanting to identify himself or herself with his success.

Well, here are 5 habits of Bill Gates:

1. **He Is Generous**

The 65-year-old founder of Microsoft Corporation is by no means a mean person (pun intended). He has donated to charity drives uncountable times. Many students are beneficiaries of his generosity through the Bill & Melinda Gates Foundation. He has come out strongly to support the education of black and Latino students, and those experiencing poverty in the United States.

Bill Gates – co-chair and trustee of Bill & Melinda Gates Foundation – has committed over $1.75 billion over two years for Covid-19 pandemic relief. He, besides Mackenzie Scott, Warren Buffet, and George Soros are among the wealthiest most generous people.

He understands perfectly that to him who much is given, much will be expected. The world is full of praises for the generosity of the world's fourth-richest person. His foundation is the world's largest charitable foundation and he has not stopped at that. To the father of three, poverty eradication is one of his life-long goals.

We can take a cue from him and start giving to receive. We should not always be the recipients of charities. Learn to give, not out of abundance but out of the love for humanity.

2. He Treasures His Family

It is an open secret that the father of three is a family man. It is amazing how he has been able to keep his family together all those years despite his wealth. Until May 4th 2021, Bill was married to Melinda. In a statement sent to the BBC, they said it was regrettable that they had to end their 27-year-old marriage. Nevertheless, his contribution to keeping his family close to his chest cannot be ignored.

He has not allowed his family affairs to come out to the public. Even when he divorced his wife in May 2021, they issued a joint statement to the media and kept their divorce under wraps. This is unlike the noisy and messy divorces that most celebrities have.

We learn from Bill Gates the importance of family. It is always God first and family next. Treasure your family because blood is always thicker than water. Whenever there is conflict, do not let it spill out to the public but sort it out amicably.

3. He Is A Social Man

From public appearances in social functions to corporate events, Bill Gates does not shy away from the public. He takes his time to attend personally to matters that require his presence. He has learned not to build a fortress or isolate himself.

With the type of publicity he receives, a man of his stature would naturally want to lead a quiet life and focus primarily on his businesses. However, he has a strong online presence. Be it LinkedIn, Twitter, Instagram, or Facebook, he shares his thoughts fearlessly.

Moreover, the technology giant founder engages captains of industry in meaningful and fruitful conversations. He has embraced the human nature of socializing and talking to people. Likewise, we should follow in tow. We should not live in fortresses because we will be cut off from the outside world and that will be the beginning of our downfall.

Attend that lunch or dinner with your colleagues, go to the graduation party of your associates, attend birthday parties and weddings. It is these social events and more that will link you with potential destiny connectors and you will grow your network. Your network is your net worth.

4. He Is Conscious of His Public Image

Bill Gates has created for himself an image of a calm and composed leader. Dressed in smart elegant suits for every occasion, the multibillionaire never fails to impress. Not once can you fault the man over his dress code. Have you ever heard of the saying "dress how you want to be addressed?"

Your dressing speaks volumes as to the kind of person you are. Dressing in itself is an art. Carefully observe not to underdress or overdress because it sends an unspoken message to those you meet.

Never has the 65-year-old billionaire been involved in a public saga. He is careful to carry himself with decorum whenever he is in public. Public perception is key to maintain his social stature – an art he has perfected over the years. Even the speech he gives is in tandem with his public image.

The thought that Bill Gates can speak rumors or even argue in public is unfathomable. He is a towering icon of success and is careful not to belittle his image. It takes a lifetime to build a reputation but a few minutes to ruin it completely.

5. He Has A Progressive Mindset

It all begins from the mind. Our mindset is what makes us stand out. It is easier for Bill Gates to be content with what he has achieved so far. He made history as the youngest American billionaire at 31 years until Zuckerberg broke that record in 2010.

He has received numerous accolades and awards for his work, but he is still not content at that level. This does not mean that Bill is ungrateful. He is grateful. It is only that he has set his mind on much higher targets. That is the progressive mindset all of us ought to emulate.

Most people fall into the trap of settling down for less in the name of being altruistic. It is time to stop getting comfortable and borrow a page from the lifestyle of Bill. The mind is where reason is born. Bill Gates knows this perfectly well and despite his wealth and achievements, he keeps moving forward.

Bill's progressive mindset has made him grow his corporation to become the world's biggest company with a valuation of $1 trillion. It begins and ends with the mind.

The above are 5 habits of Bill Gates that he has developed over time. They have made him who he is today.

Chapter 7:
10 Habits of Jack Ma

It takes a special person to amass a total net worth of more than $20 billion through hard work and keeping a sense of perspective. Alibaba, one of world's largest e-commerce online platforms, Ceo and founder, Jack Ma is one of the world's wealthiest people, but his success hasn't clouded his strategic direction. Jack Ma's success habits will truly inspire you whether you are an aspiring billionaire or you're a small-business entrepreneur.

To grow his e-commerce business, Jack overcame all difficulties. He had a rough upbringing in communist China. He also failed the college admissions exams twice and was turned down by more than a dozen businesses. He had previously created two failed Internet businesses. However, the third time, Alibaba took off swiftly.

Here are 10 things you can grasps from Jack Ma success journey:

1. Giving Up is Failing

Jack Ma is one person who understands the meaning of failure, as it started in his early days. He founded two companies which terribly failed before the success of Alibaba. For Ma, giving up is failure.

Give your grind your best shot even when the struggle is real. Failing shouldn't make you give up, instead make sure you see the goal through to the end. Hardship is your learning lesson, and understanding its lessons is the key to fortune.

2. Let Your Initiative Impact on Society Positively

Ma created his vision focusing on its impactful influence on consumers. He also notes that consumer's happiness should be the end goal rather than the profits.

Let your entrepreneurial path be the reason why people's lives are improving. This results will be in long-term-positive business relationships.

3. What's Matters Is Where You Finish

Your humble beginnings shouldn't prevent you from taking chances. Your spirit, toughness, grit, and fortitude will tell whether or not you'll succeed.

What matters is whether you are putting much effort as needed and this will tell how determined you are to succeed. Dig in your heels, like Jack Ma, and give every opportunity your all.

4. Act Swiftly

According to Jack Ma, you must be extremely quick in seizing opportunities. To win in the end, you must first be off the starting line. You must also be quick to recover from and learn from mistakes. Grab an opportunity that is in your line of sight as soon as you see it and work with it before anyone else does. This will elevate you above your competitors, who are merely competent.

5. Persistence

Ma believes that leaders must be tenacious and with a clear vision. Understanding what you want and having the drive to pursue it will not only put you on the path to success, but will also inspire those around you to work hard to achieve their goals. Ma's business concept is around taking pleasure in one's job and refusing to accept no for an answer.

6. Foresightedness

A good leader, according to Jack Ma, should have foresight. As a leader, it's good that you're always one step ahead of the competition by anticipating how decisions will be implemented before others. Invest your time in developing creative strategies while intensifying a trait where you always follow a knowledge-based intuition.

7. Take a risk

Ma founded Alibaba Group, a very successful conglomerate of internet enterprises, in the face of skepticism from potential investors. The perfect time to take risks, is when you are pursuing your chosen goal path-when criticism is at its core.

8. Be Prepared to Fail

Jack Ma is no stranger to failure. He applied to college three times before being accepted. He created two unsuccessful companies before success of Alibaba. Even KFC didn't think he was a good fit.
When you give up on your first try, you are turning your life around. As probably you'll move on to something else while ending your dreams.

9. Take Chances When You're Still Young

Ma believes that if you are not wealthy by the age of 35, you have squandered your youth. Take use of your youth's vitality and imagination by succumbing to your goal and pursuing it.

Accept and learn from every opportunity that comes your way while you're still young. Grab every opportunity and make best of it by giving it your all. Your ability to pick up any job will help you develop tenancy.

10. Live life

Ma has a reputation for not taking things too seriously. Despite his hectic schedule, he always finds time to relax and enjoy life. If you work your whole life, you will undoubtedly come to regret it.

Conclusion

Jack Ma is one of most inspiring person in the world. His struggle way up and desire for wealth continues to inspire. Through his experience, Jack Ma demonstrates how as an entrepreneur, you can bring ambition to life.

Chapter 8:
10 Habits of Bernard Arnault

Bernard Arnault- French investor, businessman, and CEO of LVMH recently reclaimed the title "worlds' wealthiest" from fellow billionaire Jeff Bezos. His business acumen and awe-inspiring financial achievements deserve to be recognized. His perspective can serve as a model for entrepreneurs who want to follow in his footsteps.

Bernard Arnault has written about money, prosperity, leadership, and power over the years. Moreover, his path to becoming the CEO of one of the world's most recognized brands will provide you with valuable lessons to emulate from. That is, your life circumstances shouldn't stop you from expanding and thriving outside your expertise.

Following his impressive accomplishments, here are ten points you can take away from Arnault's journey to success.

1. Happiness Before Money

According to Bernard, happiness is leading. That is leading your team to the top whether you are in business, sports, music industry. Money, according to him, is a consequence, and success is a blend of your past and future.

Your priority is not what you'll make sooner! When you put much-required effort into your job, profits will flow.

2. Mistakes Your Lesson

Your biggest mistake is your learning opportunity. When your business isn't performing well, understand the situation first and be patient.

In the world of innovative brands, it can take years to get something to work. Give it time and put yourself in a long-term expectation.

3. Always Behave as a Startup

Think small. Act quickly. Smaller boats can turn faster than more giant tankers. Arnault emphasizes the significance of thinking small. LVMH, in Arnault's opinion, is not a massive corporation device with miles of unnecessary bureaucracy.

Believe in your vision while attracting the best talent for your success path. A handy, adaptable speed, one that can fail quickly as easy to sleeve up.

4. Continuously Reinvent Yourself

How do you maintain your relevance? Bernard's LVMH is built on innovation, quality, entrepreneurship, and, essentially, on long-term vision. LVMH excels at developing increasingly desirable new products and selling them globally.
To be successful today, with your capabilities, opt for a worldwide startup and see what's going on. This necessitates a more considerable investment, which gives you an advantage. However, let the Creators run your inventions.

5. Team-Creative Control

Arnault strategies find creative control under each product's team to do what they do best. Arnault's designers are the dreamer's realists and critics. Allow your team to take creative control. You risk putting a tourniquet around their minds if you restrict them in any way.

6. Create Value To Attract Customers

Marketing investigates what the customer desires. As a result, you are doing what they need: creating a product and testing it to see if it works. Keeping your products in close contact with consumers, according to Arnault, makes a desire to buy in them. LVMH creates products that generate customers. For him, it's never about sales; it's always about creating desire. Your goal should be to be desirable for long-term marketability.

7. Trust the Process

There will always be different voices in business, and while there will undoubtedly be good advice, if you believe an idea will succeed, you may need to persevere until the end. Like Arnault, disregard your critics by following through with your vision to excel.

8. Your Persistence Is Everything

It would be best if you were very persistent. It would be best to have ideas, but the idea is only 20% of the equation. The execution rate is 80%. So if you are trying out a startup, having ideas marvellous, the driving force is persistence and execution.

When it comes to the most successful startups, such as Facebook, the idea was great from the beginning. Others, however, had the same idea. So why is Facebook such a phenomenal success today? It is critically through execution with persistence.

9. Do Not Think of Yourself

Bernard Arnault can be differentiated from other billionaires like Elon Musk or Bill Gates by focusing on the brands, making their longevity rather than making himself the face. He is only concerned with promoting his products.

To accomplish this, you must maintain contact with pioneers and designers, for example, while also making their ideas more specific and sustainable.

10. Maintain Contact With Your Company

One of the most common leadership mistakes is to lose sight of the company once you reach the top and "stick" with manageable goals. Instead, to see if the machine is working correctly or if there is room for improvement, you must examine every corner and every part of it.

Conclusion

Your willingness to outwork and your ability to outlearn everyone will keep your success journey intact and going. Bernard Arnault's path to becoming the CEO of the worlds most recognized and desired multi-billion empire of brands have a valuable lesson for you: your starting point does not influence or determine your future destination.

Chapter 9:
8 Habits You Should Have For Life

The key to being happy, feeling energized, and having a productive life relies on a cycle of good habits. Achieving a state of spiritual and physical satisfaction is a conscious choice that you can make for yourself. Realize what attaining the greatest happiness means for you and strive to be as productive as you can to achieve that happiness. Work towards a sense of self-realization and start reaching for your goals one step at a time. Accomplishing this requires you to be confident and have a sense of self, built entirely on good habits. This includes having good attitudes, thoughts, and decision-making skills. Quoting the all-time favorite Poet-

Maya Angelou, "a good life is achieved by liking who you are, what you do, and how you do it."

How do you put this in place? Living by good habits and discipline nourishes your potential and make you a better person in your surroundings.

Here are 8 habits you should adopt for life:

1. **Create a clear Morning Routine That Is Non-Negotiable.**

Creating a morning routine that you like and living up to it is essential. Before you start your day, you can turn to what you like doing be it running, meditating, or having a peaceful meal-time at breakfast. Whatever activities you choose based on your liking, kick start your day with that habit. Managing your morning routine and making it a habit enables you to start your day on a proactive and positive note. This will also help you in enhancing your mental health and productivity. Through trial and error find out what works best for you and stick to you day in and out.

2. **Make a Point of Physically Exercising Your Body Muscles.**

To jog your cognitive skills, relieve stress that has a hold on your performance stamina means that you need to exercise-go to the gym regularly or as much as you can. Do you still need more convincing reasons for hitting the gym? Here you go! Physical exercises increase your 'happy' moods chemically and propels the release of hormone endorphins. This hormone aids in getting rid of all the body and mind anxious feelings, hence enabling you to calm down.

3. Develop Quality Personal Relationships With Loved Ones.

The Harvard [study of adult development](#) has found that most of the existing long-term happiness for an individual is predicted through healthy relationships. Developing and maintaining close relationships with your loved ones or those close to people you consider family has been found to help someone live a longer and quality life. Hence it is the connections within your surroundings that make your life worthwhile.

4. Master an Attitude of Listening.

If you want to cultivate relationships in your life, be it professional or personal, communication is key. While communicating with your peers, family, or colleagues, you need to understand that listening to what they are saying is important. This is because you cannot have effective communication if it's one-sided. Remember that it is always important to value what others have to say. Their perspective might impact you, but most importantly, when you listen, you make others feel valued. Always try to understand the other party's point of view even if it defers from yours. Be open-minded to differing opinions. The more you listen, the more you get to learn.

5. Choose Natural Food Rather Than Processed Ones To Help Keep Your Brain Intact.

Whatever we eat always impacts our health, energy, moods, and concentration level. Whether you have weight issues or not, eating a healthy diet is essential. First off, the normality of having a healthy breakfast, lunch, or dinner is an act of practicing self-esteem and self-love. Therefore, eating healthy will always boost your self-esteem, lessen emotional issues, and your daily productivity will eventually be taken care of. If you choose to put unhealthy food in your body, you are not protecting the sanctuary that is giving you life. Make a conscious effort tot choose foods that give you the best chance of success, health, and wellness. As we all know, money can't buy health.

6. Be Appreciative More Than You Are Disparaging

Mastering the art of gratitude is a great way to live a happy, stress-free, healthy, and fulfilling life. As French writer Alphonse said: "We can complain because rose plants have thorns or we can rejoice as thorns also have roses." It's always easy to forget how fortunate you are while trying to push through life and the obstacles that come along with it. How do you master this art? Start a journal of appreciation to be grateful for the things you have. Take the time to appreciate those closest to you, those who care about you, and remember at least one good thing about yourself each and every day. Don't forget to make a note of what you have accomplished as well before you go to bed. The more you take notice of the little joys in life, the happier you will be.

7. Be With a Circle of Friends That Are Positive Minded.

Be careful about who you spend your precious time and energy with. A happy life can be contagious if we know where to attract it. Coincidentally, happiness is also the easiest way to develop positivity in our lives. With that in mind, choose to surround yourself which such people who will bring light into your world. Spend time with those who will nurture you each step of the way and don't hesitate to let go of the people who are eating away at your energy and spirits. Let's not forget the wise words of entrepreneur Jim Rohn, "You are the five people you spent the most time averagely. You only live once! Let it be worthwhile.

8. Take Breaks Regularly To Invest in Self-Care.

Although you might be very passionate about your work and your daily schedules, it is okay to take some time - an hour, minute, second, or even a day off. If you take a while to unwind, you will do wonderful things for your mood, mind, and self-esteem. Spend some time doing at least one thing that makes you feel good every day – whether it be listening to music, engaging in sports, starting a new hobby, dabbling in the arts, or even simply preparing a pleasant meal for yourself, you deserve to do it. Whatever floats your boat, don't neglect it!

Conclusion

Determination, persistence, and continuous effort are essential for the development of these habits. It can take just a few weeks or maybe more than a year to develop your habits, so long as you don't stop. It does not matter how long it takes.

What are you waiting for? Pull up your socks; it's your time to win at life.

www.ingramcontent.com/pod-product-compliance
Lightning Source LLC
Chambersburg PA
CBHW071739080526
44588CB00013B/2091